HALLOWED BE THIS HOUSE

Harold Shaw Publishers books by Thomas Howard

CHANCE OR THE DANCE?:
A Critique of Modern Secularism

CHRIST THE TIGER

HALLOWED BE THIS HOUSE

Hallowed Be This House

Thomas Howard

Harold Shaw Publishers
Wheaton, Illinois

Previously published as SPLENDOR IN THE ORDINARY First Harold Shaw Publishers printing, July, 1979

Library of Congress Catalog Number 79-64947

ISBN 0-87788-786-1

Printed in the United States of America

For my sister Elisabeth,
who is a pattern of *caritas* for me

1

The ancients used to hallow places. They set aside groves and grottoes and mountains, and built temples and shrines and enclaves. Places mattered to them. They thought that a place could be fenced off and acknowledged to be the dwelling of the god, or the spot where the god had done some memorable thing. Here was a holy well, and there was an oracle. Here was an altar, and there was a tabernacle. The landscape of antiquity is dotted with these things, and it is natural that it should be. If the gods are there, and if their influence touches our realm, then memorable things are going to happen, and we men do well to mark off the precincts. Otherwise somebody might step across a line he ought not to step across, or cut down a tree that is not available for lumber, and end up paying with his life for having missed his cues.

This is all strange to us later men, or at least quaint. We know better than to think that there are any gods about, much less gods that can be pinned down to places. If we do believe in a god—or God, shall we say—he is certainly not the sort of being who can be *housed*. He is everywhere. His Spirit, like the wind, blows where it will. We cannot wall him into a shrine or pen him in an oak. He fills all things, and if he dwells anywhere, it is in the hearts of people who love him.

At this point, Christians (who, unlike most twentieth-century men, share with the ancients at least the idea that we do live and walk in the presence of the unseen) are assenting. We do acknowledge and worship such a God. He has entered our history; indeed he is the Lord of our history and has acted dramatically in that history. But he has told us that his dwelling is not in temples made with hands but rather in the heaven of heavens—and "with him also that is of a contrite and humble spirit."

Hence Christians think more about God in their hearts than God in a temple. No matter what holy places there are for Christians (and some give more weight to this than others), any Christian, when the chips are down, knows that his own body, like that of Mary, is God's earthly sanctuary. It is to this temple that a Christian must give his most serious attention. It is more important for this to be swept and attended to than for the church building to be tidy (although there is, of course, no either/or situation: devout Christians tend to keep their churches, like their selves, clean).

Not only because of this inner focus in Christianity, but also because we modern men, Christian or nonreligious, live under the scientific myth which tells us that everything is explainable sooner or later and hence that there are no "divine mysteries" about—because of this, modern Christians often find it difficult to keep alive any notion at all of mystery, or of the hallowed, except perhaps as a sort of cloud or glow that ought to suffuse their imagination when they pray or worship. It is hard to see ourselves as walking daily among the hallows—that is, as carrying on the commonplace routines of our ordinary life in the presence of mighty mysteries that would ravish and terrify us if this veil of ordinariness were suddenly stripped away.

Take something like getting meals, for example. This is one of these commonplace routines. We do it three times a day, more or less, and we are probably thinking mainly of getting the Rice Krispies box open, or the plastic off the bologna, or the frozen spinach into the saucepan. There is no religious mumbo jumbo that attends the getting of meals. We would look blankly at anyone who suggested that we were doing something eucharistic there on the formica altar in the kitchen. What? Eucharistic? And yet we are. The point is that we have never thought of it that way. We sing in church to a God who dwells "in light inaccessible hid from our eyes," and who was also known to his followers in the breaking of bread. But never in a thousand mealtimes does it occur to us that he can be known in our ordinary, daily breaking of bread. That's only in church, and there it isn't literal anyway. We're just getting breakfast here. What do you mean, eucharistic?

Or again, going off to work on an ordinary morning, say. This activity is set about with starting the car and coping with traffic and parking and one harassing thing and another, and it certainly has nothing to do with these hallows we were speaking of. Maybe there was a time back at the beginning of history when life was simple and Eden-like, and man could still see that his daily work had something to do with the whole rhythm of life, and could offer up the labor of his hands to God as a sacrifice. But that has long since disappeared, and it would be plain superstition to suppose that driving a steam shovel or floating a loan or taking minutes in a board meeting had anything to do with offerings to God. We make our offerings in church when the plate comes past.

Or again, take something daily and ordinary like raising children. Of course we want them eventually to know and love God, and we teach them and take them to church and so forth. But all this daily clutter of potty chairs and toys and rubbers and earaches and one thing and another—this is just hurly-burly. It's because of all this stuff that we can never get around to the real business. All this clutter keeps us on the chase and never allows us time to breathe and think and *live* with our children. They inhabit the same house as we do, but we end up being mere laundresses and chauffeurs and umpires for them. If there was ever a simple time in history when parenthood and childhood could be carried on the way it was all supposed to be done, it has gone with the wind.

Somehow we have gotten swept into a millrace, and it's nonstop flailing and thrashing just to keep ourselves from drowning. The sheer necessities of modern life sweep us farther and farther from any sense that it is all hallowed, really. What are we to do?

There are various things we could do no doubt. We could resign ourselves to the millrace and abandon any thought of anything but the flailing. Or we could take some drastic step like moving to a farm in Vermont or an island in the Aegean, hoping thereby to find some peace and quiet where

11

we would be able to recollect ourselves and do things right. A third possibility would be to accept the fact that life comes tumbling at us nowadays but that it is nonetheless possible for us to see our ordinary daily routines as proceeding among the hallows, so to speak; and by stirring up in our minds the things that we vaguely acknowledge anyway, to begin to hallow those routines by doing once more what men have always done with things to hallow them; namely, offering them up in oblation to God, as literally as Abel offered up sacrifices from his ordinary routine of work.

The point is, despite the changes in the scenery from one age to another, the drama itself does not change. God is still the Most High God, and our life is still set about with blissful and terrible mysteries, and sacrifice is still at the center of things; and we (all of us—Abel, Solomon, and we modern men) are bidden to offer sacrifices.

The trouble is, of course, that it all gets squeezed into a corner in this pell-mell of TV and urban and suburban living and one thing and another. We shift the Big Things (sacrifice, mystery, the hallowed) over onto the "religious" shelf and tie it up with church services, alms, and prayers. Alas, we say, we don't have the simplicity that Abel knew, or the panoply that Solomon knew. It would be easy with those circumstances to keep alive a vision of everything as hallowed. But it is impossible in our secularist hurry to do this. Somehow splendor, mystery, and terror don't show up in the fabric of our life.

It is the argument of this book that this will not do. Admittedly we do live in an epoch when the general shape and hue of things makes it *nearly* impossible. But we will have allowed ourselves to be bilked if we take up with this despairing atheism, for that is what it is, really. The "secularization" of life urged on us by science and commerce and modernity generally is surely one of the bleakest myths ever to settle down over men's imagination.

And it is the argument of this book that we do, in fact, walk daily among the hallows; and that our task now is exactly what Abel's or Solomon's was; namely, to offer whatever we do have, in the presence of the divine mysteries, as a continual oblation. To do this, of course, we will have to recover the sense of the hallowed as being all around us. We will have to open our eyes and try to see once more the commonplace as both cloaking and revealing the holy to us. We will have to refuse resolutely the secularism that has made ordinariness unholy. We live in a dark age, and somewhere in this murk there have got to be lights burning in shrines and on altars, bearing witness to the presence of the holy.

But what shrines and altars? The Philistines of

our own times have thrown them all down and defiled everything.

I would like to suggest that at least one place (among others) which may be hallowed anew as the place where the celebration of all the mysteries may occur, and where all of life may be offered up in oblation to the Most High, is the family household. Within these four walls, under this roof, the lamps are lighted. The offering is here, the vigil is here, the feast is here, the faithful are here. All the eating and drinking, and the working and playing, and the discipline and serving and loving that go on here—they are all holy. For these common routines of ordinary life are not only necessities and functions: they are also messengers to us from the hallows. Nay, more than messengers, they *are* those hallows, set hourly before us in visible, touchable, light-of-day forms.

How "hallows"? The word itself is out of date. It sounds spooky.

But any Christian, and any orthodox Jew, and any pagan with his images, for that matter, knows that what lies about him in his ordinary routines does, in fact, speak of more than its immediate function. It opens out onto vistas that stretch beyond our seeing, into the realm of mystery. Human bodies, for instance, are somehow images of God; work has something to do with our role as lords of creation; eating is a physical case in point of the nourishment that our inner man needs; sleep is a small metaphor of death; and so forth. Ordinariness, in a word, opens out onto mystery, and the thing that men are supposed to do with mystery is to hallow it, for it all belongs to the Holy One.

The family household, then, is at least one obvious place where we may come upon the hallows in very ordinary terms. We may, by going from room to room in this place, discover what those terms look like, and how they are celebrated from day to day.

2

The door first. All houses have doors of one sort or another—a rattan mat across an opening, bronze portals swung on marble, or a plain panel of pine just like the twenty other panels set in the row of brick lining the street.

But whatever it looks like, the door is the entrance into the holy place. It is the point where "outside" abuts on "inside." Outside it is anybody's territory; inside we come to a specific place. A special order obtains in here. What that order looks like we shall have to see by being taken through the place.

But first, the door is closed. That, surely, is a wrong start? Doesn't that imply some defensiveness or exclusiveness about this place, or a fortress mentality? If that is the sort of shrine this is, we'll move on.

Some closed doors may imply this, but not this one. The very nature of a holy place is that it is different, and set apart, from what surrounds it. Borders and veils and doors have always marked holy places. There is a paradox here, of course: if what goes on inside a holy place has any validity at all, then it will flow out and hallow everything else, and that would seem to need an open door. But on the other hand, outside things must be excluded, not in the sense of consigning them to worthlessness, but of furnishing for them a place to which they can be brought and from which blessing can flow out to them.

You can see this, for example, in the Tabernacle in ancient Israel. The area where the tent stood was fenced off and veiled in and set about with terror and smoke and fire. You could not get in at all without blood sacrifice, and then only into the outer precincts; and the innermost recesses were so terrible that the High Priest alone could get in there, and that only once a year with blood, and even then he was in dire peril. But did this fencing off leave everything else *out?* Did it imply that here alone in Israel could we find anything real and worthy? On the contrary: the Tabernacle was set in the middle of the camp of Israel, and the whole notion was that there would be a ceaseless coming and going in and out of that holy place. It was not that the ordinary life of Israel—their cooking and washing and their haggling and packing and unpacking—was peripheral, and that they only got down to business when they brought their lambs and bullocks to the priests. It was the other way around: their bringing of their sacrifices and offerings was the *token* of the mystery that was at work through the whole fabric of their life; namely, that everything belonged to God and was therefore hallowed. The lamb brought to the door of the tent was precisely a token. In him there was gathered up and borne all the rest of their flocks, and all of their possessions, and their very lives. In other words, the presence of the fenced-off place in the middle of the camp proclaimed what was true all through that camp and to its outermost perimeter: everything was "holiness unto the Lord."

Perhaps in some ideal realm (heaven in fact is described this way in St. John's Apocalypse), we wouldn't need to have special places like this to remind us of what it is all about, since we would be gloriously able to see all the time and everywhere the holiness of things. We would need no special precincts since the whole realm would be seen to be hallowed. We would need no special times since every hour of every day would be the hour of sacrifice. We would need to bring no special offerings as tokens, since our very selves and all our work would be continuously offered up in perpetual oblation.

But alas, we aren't made that way. Or rather, we *are* made that way, but through our own fault we have marred everything. We chose (in Eden) *not* to offer things up to the Holy One but rather to grab them for ourselves, and thereby we desecrated them, turning what was given to us to secular (that is to say, unhallowed) uses. Since we can't do that in the holy place, we had to be turned out; and now we have to cope with the limitations imposed on us by our exile. Inside there, we had the capacity to live, always seeing with unblurred clarity the holiness of things. Now we have to come at it in fits and starts, helped along by special times and places and disciplines which remind us of what is really true; namely, that there is nothing that is not holy. We have a hard time keeping this vision alive, and we have to pluck ourselves by the sleeve, so to speak, in order to stay awake to the fact that we do walk among the hallows. The secular, or the profane, which is how we usually think of our ordinariness, is actually holiness unrecognized.

Hence the closed door. It is not so much saying, "Stay outside there, all you unwashed," as "There is an inside here, protected from mere randomness and clutter, in which things begin to be set in their proper order and seen in their true light." This door is for closing and for opening. To slam a door in the face of a suppliant is not the same act as closing the door after you as you welcome the stranger in from the tempest. In both cases a door has closed, though. In the former, it was a sign of hell, that is, the attitude that says, "I'll have my things and damn your need." In the latter, it was a sign of heaven, that is, the attitude that says, "Here. What we have is for you." There has to be a "here"—a special place fenced off from indeterminateness—before the host can say, "Come in here." You can't invite somebody into a generality.

So the closed door. We close the door behind ourselves and our guest, leaving weather and violence and generality outside. What have we come into?

We have come into the place where it is said to us, "You are the attendants at this shrine. See to it that what goes on here is a small picture of what ought to go on everywhere. It doesn't go on everywhere, but your task is to see that it does here. This is the spot allotted to your priesthood. Be faithful."

And as is true of any holy place, this one has for its activity the marking and celebrating of what is true, and the keeping alive of the vision of what is true; namely, that all is holy. This is done by offering things up in acts of consecration and praise. This is what lifts those things from the heap of mere ordinariness and makes them extraordinary (holy). They *are* ordinary things, of course, like eating and drinking and working and playing and bread and wine; but it is the ordinary stuff lifted up which *is* the holy. Holy things, for the Christian and the Jew in any case, aren't some remote category of things—mumbo jumbos, arcane regalia, or basalt meteorites from the sky. Holy things are ordinary things perceived in their true light, that is, as bearers of the divine mysteries and glory to us. Looked at this way, eating becomes eucharistic, and working becomes the *opus dei*, and loving becomes an image of the City of God. It is our task in this shrine to take these ordinary things and, by lifting them up in oblation, to hallow them to the service for which they were given to us here, which was to bring us to the habitation of God where we are set free to live in the splendor where eating and drinking and working and playing are known for what they really are, forms of perpetual worship and therefore bliss.

3

When you come through the door, you find yourself inside the place bounded by the four walls. What do they mean? Are they defensive walls, thrown up against the assault of outsiders?

No, no more than the door was shut against the outsiders, and no more than the flimsy curtain of skins and linen that surrounded the Tabernacle in Israel was seen as a defense against assault. That curtain was there to mark the place where a particular thing was occurring. It set the bounds. Inside, the priests went about their task, which was to bring the whole life of Israel into specially vivid focus. They weren't doing something *else*—something secret and dark and remote from daily life. The rite was simply their daily life taken and set forth in tokens and lifted up in the offerings of sacrifice and praise.

But we may ask further about that daily life and that rite. Why was it done *this* way? Why all this bloodshed? That may have been appropriate to the imagination of a primitive tribe in the desert, but there certainly would be nothing in a rite like that to correspond to our modern life; so doesn't the example of the Tabernacle break down?

No. The mysteries have not changed, at least as far as Christians are concerned. The mystery which was supposed to be at work in the life of Israel (as opposed to what was celebrated among the Hittites and the Amorites, say) and which was made present to them in the rite in the Tabernacle, was the mystery upon which all life proceeds and which will never be outgrown since it is there at the root of all things. It is the mystery of My Life For Yours. It is expressed in the words "I owe my life to you, and I lay down my life for you."

No one has ever drawn a single breath on any other basis. No child has ever received life to begin with without a "laying down" of life by the two people to whom he owes his conception, and by the laying down of his mother's life for months in bearing and nourishing him. And somebody had to lay down his life for the child year after year in caring for him and training him and providing for him. And no one has ever sat down to the smallest pittance of food that he did not owe to somebody's life having been laid down, if it was only a prawn or a lettuce leaf; to say nothing of the work (a form of laid-down life) somebody had to do to plant and cultivate and pick and market the leaf, or catch the prawn. No one has ever learned a single thing that he did not owe to somebody's having taught him or helped him one way or another. Morning, noon, and night, we owe it all to others. My Life For Yours. I owe my life to you, and I lay mine down for you.

It was this, true for Israel as it is for every people whether they acknowledge it or not, that was kept present to their imagination by the rite going on in their midst. Their ordinary life was hallowed by this perpetual acknowledgment that it was *God* to whom they finally owed everything since it was from him that it had all come to begin with. The slaying of the token victims and the pouring out of blood signalled dramatically to them that the laying down of one life for another, on which all life depends and which may take a hundred small forms during the course of a day (helping a man get his ox out of a ditch, or holding a car door open, or letting that person go first)—this laying down of life always entails a death. It is death, in effect, to *my* ten minutes when I give them over to helping you get your hapless ox back on his feet; it is death

24

to your convenience for five seconds while you hold this door for me; it is death to his privilege if he lets you cut in here ahead of him.

These little layings-down of life were understood to be cases in point of the principle which is at the root of all existence, this principle of exchanged life. Indeed, it was only by the poured-out blood of another, interposed between them and their sins, that they lived at all; and hence they had the Great Fact of all human life dramatized in their midst; and they anticipated thereby the one "full, perfect, and sufficient sacrifice, oblation, and satisfaction, for the sins of the whole world" which was to occur centuries later.

In order for this rite to be carried out, it had to occur somewhere. Of course it was at work all through the fabric of their lives. But they had to do something specific in order to rouse themselves to the thing that was already true in any case; namely, that the My Life For Yours principle is the only one on which any life at all is possible. So they drew a perimeter around a place and set it in the midst of their life.

This is what the walls of a true household are all about. They are a boundary. "Boundary" is the same word as "bond." What is the bond here? Are families prisoners to each other? Is this a jail?

When we speak of bonds and binding, we may mean imprisonment, of course. A slave is bound to his master; a captive people is bound to her captors; a criminal is bound in his fetters; a man is bound by a destructive habit.

But used in another way, the word "bond" takes on an opposite meaning. This occurs when we are talking about the bond of love. All of a sudden the grim suggestions of the word vanish. A lover's bonds are his wings. He is set free by entering into the bond of love. The arms of his beloved around him are as wide as the girdle of the world. Here in this narrow cell he has found all the empires and hemispheres that conquerors and navigators have ever sought.

And, as is true with romantic love with its bonds of glorious liberty, so it is with all the other kinds of love—connubial love, maternal love, paternal love, filial love, and so forth: the bond that ties us to someone we love is a form of liberty to us. It is as strong as death, but it is the very fountainhead of our life. (The situations where these bonds begin to chafe—where we find domestic quarrels, children running away, and divorce—are the situations where love has, precisely, receded. Boredom, irritation, disenchantment, or wrath have replaced it. Then, of course, family bonds become fetters indeed.)

The walls of the house signify the boundary enclosing the particular place where these few people are engaged in enacting the rite of love;

that is, of exchanged life. They experience it under many forms: the love of the parents for each other is one form; the love of the mother for her son, say, is another, and for her daughter another; and the father for his daughter and for his son; and the older brother for the younger sister, or the older sister for the younger brother. There are a dozen variations on the theme, but the same theme; namely, that we find real life where mutual responsibility and commitment turn out to be forms of joy. It is love that liberates the participants for this. Love sets them free from the calculating and jockeying and tallying up of scores that we find in mere politics, where we have to protect people with half-measures like equality and rights and self-determination. Love opens onto a vastly more splendid order of things; and the forms of love at work in an ordinary family are like introductions to this splendor.

This family bond is there in the fabric of ordinary human life, giving us all this chance to participate in the Real Thing. All forms of love furnish this chance in one way or another, of course—love for one's country, or for one's community, or one's master or friend. Wherever love operates, there we find some exhibition of the principle. But the obvious place where we find the natural occasion for the whole race to enact the rite is the household—in other words, in the biological family.

No one supposes that these four or five or six people are a select breed, tailored to get along with each other perfectly, or picked because they are better than anyone else. Rather, it is as though the great lesson in love which we must all learn sooner or later has been made obvious, easy, and natural by being carried along in the arms of sheer biology. It is easier and more obvious and natural for six people bound this way to learn the lessons than for six people who are trying to set up a commune, say, to learn the same thing. The commune is a brave experiment, but the wheels drive heavily eventually. Ask anyone who has ever experienced both scenes for a long time.

The walls of the house signal to us the place, then, where the rite is occurring. It is a holy place, for in it the sacred mysteries are celebrated: the mysteries of love transfiguring duty into joy, and of laid-down life understood as the principle of all life, and of ordinariness hallowed by being offered up in oblation to the Giver of every good thing.

4

There is more in a house than just walled-in space. There are rooms here. The rite which is celebrated here is a manifold rite, and the different rooms signal to us the variations in the rite.

The entryway (some houses have a real hall, but it is the same thing) is first. It is a space for passing through. We are always *en route* when we are in the entryway, either coming in or going out. There is no fixed household routine that is designed to take place in the entryway, only this coming and going. If we ever sit down there, it is only to wait for someone.

But coming and going are major activities of life. The Hebrews were on to something when they sang, "The Lord shall preserve thy going out and thy coming in." A good bit of human life is taken up with coming and going. How do we see it?

In modern houses most of the coming and going occurs through the garage into the breezeway and thence into the kitchen. The items that surround our coming and going tend to be lawn mowers, bags of turf builder, spin dryers, galoshes, jackets, and linoleum. It used to be a matter of plush chairs, little tables, mirrors, umbrella stands, and carpet—items, it might be observed, that helped to formalize and deck all this coming and going. You were almost forced to pause as you came in. You were clearly *entering* something. Even for the adolescent slamming in from school and flinging down briefcase and hat, there was the awareness (doubtless ingrained and therefore unconscious) that you had to get farther in before you let your hair down completely. For the family generally, it signalled the haven: we're home now, and home is a place full of grace and order. For the visitor it signalled the welcome, a welcome decked with beauty because a welcome is something worth decking.

In our own time, we have for the most part skirted this rite. We come in through the back door, and some even hale their guests in by this route, carrying it off with gay remarks about how they're just family anyway, so they'll feel at home.

If anyone from an earlier era, who was accustomed to front doors and entrance hallways, taxed us about this informality, our rejoinder would be that our way is much more honest. Why put up a show? Why have fake scenery? Everyone knows that a family spends most of its time in the kitchen and its precincts, so why cobble up a lot of plush trumpery and create a wholly artificial situation by bringing people through a door nobody ever uses into a room nobody ever uses? It's as though we won't welcome them into the real place.

Our interlocutor, however, might point out that, far from being fakery, the plush (or the tapestries, or the marble, or the little welcome mat, depending on what century and what income bracket we are talking about) signalled something fully as real as the spin dryer and galoshes; namely, that there are *differences of function* in a well-ordered house, and that one of the loveliest of all functions is the pompous welcome.

Pomp?

Yes, pomp. Our inability to hear this word as meaning anything other than puffery betrays our poor imagination. We have been taught a mercilessly practical dogma in which virtually all ceremony and splendor are thought to be humbug. There is no purple on the hem of our presidents' garments, for instance: they are our "chief executives," and if there is any symbol of their office at all, it is the attache case. That is something functional, not ceremonial; and function is real, whereas ceremony is fake. Or again, in academic institutions (at least in the one where I teach), it is supremely difficult to get scholars or athletes even to *stand up* in a convocation to acknowledge applause for their achievements, much less to come to the front. Instead you get hangdog smirks, as much as to say, "Forget it. Leave me alone."

This may be why we don't have front halls any more. The idea of special occasions which are worth festooning is uncomfortable to us since it looks to us as though it implies that there is something lacking in honest, everyday ordinariness. Hailing brilliant scholars or athletes, or putting on our best bib and tucker for Sunday, or welcoming guests in through the front hallway—it must mean that we think the ordinary stuff is not good enough.

But there is another way of seeing it. Can it not be said that the ordinary is *affirmed* by setting it off now and again, and decking it. For example, ordinary schoolwork well done is a worthy thing: so in hailing the scholar we affirm and dignify all studies, saying in effect to the rest of the students, "The job you are working at is a worthy one. Work, then, to do it right." If in a different situation we wanted to hail the virtue of effort, then we would celebrate the students who had tried the hardest regardless of their final achievement, and in this case we would have to exclude the lazy ones from recognition even if their marks were the highest. Of course, if there is nothing at all about studies worth hailing, then we dispense with ceremony altogether. This last is more or less the idea controlling contemporary imagination.

Or again, ordinary athletics well done is a worthy thing: so in hailing the athlete, we celebrate all athletics, saying in effect, "This achievement here is what the rest of you are working at. It is worth working at." If there is no difference between a four-minute mile and an eight-minute mile, or if the four-minute mile is no better than an eight-minute one, then by all means leave off the celebration. The laurel was simply a way we had of saying publicly 1) that achievement rather than mere effort is something worthy, and 2) that it is better to have a very finely-tuned body than a less finely-tuned one. Nobody is urging that this man here who can run a mile in four minutes is a better *man* than this man over here who totters in four minutes later. The laurel says only one thing: he is a better *runner*. He may be a cad into the bargain, and the loser may be a saint: that can be acknowledged in another ceremony.

Or it may be unhappily true, in a reverse of the hare and tortoise tale, that the hare *did* beat the worthy tortoise with no effort, while the poor tortoise put out infinitely more honest effort and lost and hence got no recognition. To correct this imbalance, we have to set up alternative celebrations hailing effort, in which case the lazy people, or the effortless ones, might quarrel, saying we are rewarding effort and who's to say *that* is anything worth celebrating. And so we are back around to a state of affairs where nobody celebrates anything for fear of discriminating. (The difficulty with this line of thought is that it fondly supposes that by dispensing with a discriminating scale of values, we will thereby allow everyone to be at the top and nobody will feel inferior; whereas the effect we actually get for our egalitarian pains is the reverse: everyone finds himself in a broil at the bottom. Hell, presumably, is such a broil: everything stirred together in a grey pudding. Nothing *better than* anything else. Everyone struggling impotently, clamoring for equal time and equal dignity.)

But hell is a long way from the back-door/front-hall question, and the suggestion here is not that those who let their guests in through the garage will go to hell. On that brisk accounting, my own number is up.

The point about one entrance or another is simply that to do it the one way (via the front entrance, say) may keep alive in our imaginations something important. To do it the other (through the garage) is not necessarily to deny this important something: it is simply to have dropped one easy and natural way of affirming it.

What is this "important something"? Isn't it at least this, that by distinguishing between one activity and another in a household, and by illuminating that distinction with such aids as customs and furniture and architecture, we clarify and hence dignify the whole enterprise? To wit: yard work is one activity, represented in the lawn mowers and turf builder. Children coming and going to and from school is another (the galoshes and jackets). Laundry is another (the spin dryer), and cooking is another (linoleum—a good floor covering for the place where grease is spilled). And entering the house and welcoming guests is still another. All of these things occur in a household. They are all parts of the rite, we might say. No one of them is unworthy. But to be obliged to carry them all on in the presence of all the others is to live in a blur (and hell, surely, is the ultimate blur?). Rubbers on the living room rug, laundry on the sideboard—it may be necessary for a minute or two, but they don't *belong* there. If we object "Why not?" it can only be rejoined that this question arises from a doubt on our part that there is any such thing at all as a proper place for things. To speak of proper places is, of course, to sound prim and schoolmarmish. But the schoolmarms weren't necessarily wrong about everything. Maybe they knew something, at least on this point. In any case, the custom of using the back door for one kind of entrance (into the kitchen with the bags from the A & P, or into the breezeway with muddy galoshes) and the front door for another (welcoming guests) is one way of distinguishing between various parts of the rite, and hence of clarifying and dignifying all the parts.

But I spoke of architecture as another aid in this distinction. Do I mean that we have to tear down our houses and build new ones with vast entrance halls, preferably with balconies for liveried heralds with silver trumpets? Well, no. But most houses have *some* sort of front door. Abraham's tent, presumably, had a flap through which he could welcome his guests (and with the set of guests Abraham had, you had to watch how you did things). The idea is, if it happens to be possible and convenient, having a front door has a purpose in it beyond the mere function of getting people through the wall.

The very dividing up of the space in a house with partitions bespeaks this distinguishing of one kind of activity from another that I am talking about. Functionally, it might be easier to have the stove by the sofa. That way the hostess could do it all simultaneously. Or the toilet by the bed. This would save a lot of nocturnal groping up and down halls. But for whatever reasons, the human imagination has not seen it this way. There seems to have been something more than function at work in this imagination.

And this "something more" is the "important something" of two paragraphs back carried further: it is the distinguishing between one activity and another, and then the decking of each activity appropriately, that is, in a form or shape corresponding to its own nature. There is nothing, for example, about the lawn mower, that wants to be set in the hall. Why not? Because besides the fact that we would be forever blundering over it, catching our hems on it, and barking our shins, the lawn mower introduces a discordant *note* into the hall. The hall is for coming and going, and for welcoming and bidding farewell. That is one part of the rite. The lawn mower is for another part of the rite—the tending of the garden, as it were. It is all part of one whole rite, and one part suffers no ignominy because it is distinguished from another. It is simply that being the sort of creatures we are, we can do things better in a sequence, and the parts of that sequence are like the notes on a scale or the colors in a spectrum: lovely when they are set in significant relationship to each other but not worth much stirred together in cacophony or smudge.

The lawn mower in the hall may be such a smudge, since it represents toil (itself a most noble part of the rite), whereas the hall represents first, pause and preparation, and second, honor. These all need to be kept distinct for any of them to appear clearly.

Pause and preparation. In any holy place, we have to be given a chance to collect our wits. It is not like falling into a seat on a bus or racing up to the newsstand counter for the paper. We feel as though we are stepping across some line from one order of activity to another, and we are quite right. When we come into temples and shrines, even if they are only vacant ruins, and ruins of a cult we ourselves don't believe in, for some reason we lower our voices and walk circumspectly. And we are quite right to do so. If we have no capacity for awe in the presence of the mysterious and the vastly other, then we are on the way to becoming churls, nothing more.

But of course this sort of religious hush and awe does not exactly apply to the entrance to houses where ordinary families live. It is not as though the visitor is asked to leave his shoes outside and put on felt slippers when he crosses the threshold, or the adolescent son to genuflect to the umbrella stand as he blows in from school. The point here is that the hall or entryway is an entirely wasted bit of space if there is nothing more to it than some idea of giving us elbow room to take off our coats. That could in a pinch be done in the living room. In so far as there is a hall, it has that practical function, plus the more elusive one of signalling to us what all vestibules and narthexes signal; namely, the brief pause and preparation before getting into the rite proper. If the rite has any meaning or weight at all—if it is a solemnity worth observing in the first place—then it is worth our while composing ourselves for it, and girding up our loins, as it were, so that we can truly "assist at" it (there is an old Christian idea of not just "being present at" the liturgy, but of *assisting at* it: this idea is kept alive in the French verb *assister à*). We don't just step through the door and find ourselves in the middle of things. Just as in any rite there is a sort of increasing intensity, from the beginning up to the high point, so we may see in the layout of houses a suggestion of the same thing: the sacred mysteries are celebrated here; pause and make your preparation, for this business of the household is a demanding rite. It encompasses all the mysteries of love.

The hall represents, then, a suggestion. It is not as though we catch our breath in awe here, any more than we catch our breath every time we go through a doorway with molding on the lintel. But the molding on the lintel originally carried with it some idea of dignifying entrances by decking them. The molding is there, silent and unobtrusive. But it is there nonetheless, a modest reminder that if we care to think about it (and far be it from the lintel to be shrill and insist), the act of anyone's entering any place is a significant act, recognized along the whole spectrum, from the great cry "Lift up your heads, O ye gates, and the King of Glory shall come in!" to the secrecy with which we surround the sexual rite. Entries are significant. In the hurry of the commonplace, of course, we can't stop over every entry, and we would be paralyzed if we were obliged to. This rhythmic balance between intensity and ordinariness seems to be necessary to us mortals who can't bear very much stark reality. We can't, for example, sustain for very long the vision of God that may be vouchsafed to us once in a long while when we pray or hear the "Te Deum." Or again, if our passion for our beloved were always as fierce as it is at the height of the rite itself, we would perish of a surfeit of bliss. We have to have *pianissimo* as well as *fortissimo*; *largo* as well as *presto*; plains as well as alps.

So it is with entrance halls and their suggestion of the mystery that is at work in all entering and leaving. They are there, built into the house; and we may be reminded of what it is all about now and again by thinking of them thus. But most of the time we come and go, as we are supposed to come and go, merely living out our ordinariness. The hall may remind us that it is an ordinariness set amongst the hallows—nay, that the ordinary *is* the hallowed.

Pause and preparation, then. But there is a second suggestion at work in the entrance hall.

This is the place where we greet and bid farewell to guests. The hall's function is to furnish a space for this. There would certainly be nothing immoral about letting guests in through the cellar. Indeed in a tempest, or if they are being pursued by brigands, they will be happy with whatever opening we let them in by. But in so far as we have ever had the leisure to rise above the merely pell-mell, we human beings have thought it appropriate to deck the business of welcome and farewell as beautifully as we can. By this decking we are saying in effect, "Hail, worthy lady. Hail, noble man. Here is our house. You are welcome. We honor your grace with the best we have."

What? What sort of antique language is that? Are we talking about twentieth-century, middle-class life, or about Agamemnon or King Arthur?

Admittedly we don't commonly use exactly these phrases. But if it is not something like this, then what *are* we doing in the act of welcome? What would we really wish to say if we had the gift of perfect utterance? If we were truly generous and courteous (which is what having guests is all about), we would want to reach for some such idea as is uttered in those old phrases.

It all has to do with seeing and honoring the excellence of the other. That is what courtesy is, in a way—the capacity to treat all other selves as though they were kings. Or put it the other way around: in the figure of a king we see a picture of what every man is if we could only see every man clearly. Royalty wears its purple and gold vicariously, we might say: that is, they bear the heavy weight of it *for us*, since we cannot all bear that weight. But any acts of courtesy and generosity towards another person (and in this case, towards our guest) spring from an idea of what is true of this one or that one; namely, that he, made as he is in the image of God, is a holy and glorious thing.

This is what is at work in the entrance hall. Admittedly it is not an area where a great deal of practical *work* goes on, not a very efficient use of space. But it bespeaks something more important perhaps than efficiency. It bespeaks an awareness of grace and glory. It sees the perpetual coming and going through the hall as a coming and going into and out of the hallowed place—hallowed because all is the gift of God to begin with; and doubly hallowed because here it is recognized as a gift, and offered up in oblation.

5

The living room is ordinarily the first real room we come into. What is it all about?

When you think about it, it is hard to isolate any specific activity that has to occur in the living room. What do we do there? Well—we sit there. When? After dinner? Who sits there? If the average household were to keep a chart showing who used the living room and for how long, we might end up with a blank. (TV time does not count, since it has no more to do with the real life of a household than a visit to the theater does.) And yet, if we were to design a house with no such room, everyone would say, "Where's the living room?"

The idea in living rooms (or family rooms, or

43

parlors, or drawing rooms) down through the centuries has been that there is an entity "the family," such that their mere being together is a good thing, and that an ordinary house will have space provided for that mere being together. There are plenty of activities that may go on in this room, of course: conversation, entertaining, games, and so forth. Virtually every one of these assumes the idea of people doing something together.

Conversation, for example. Even though this activity has fallen on dry years, we still are familiar enough with the general idea of it to know that it entails at least two people. You can't have a conversation in solitude; and you don't necessarily have a conversation when two voices happen to be going. It requires a tandem effort to get a conversation worthy of the name. People doing something together.

Or again, entertaining. Here people are brought together with the idea of letting them meet each other, enjoy each other, and enjoy the thing that is bigger than any one of them; namely, the occasion. That occasion may be nothing more than simply this getting together—"Let's have the Throckmortons and the Thistlethwaites and the Entwistles over. I think they'd enjoy each other"—and we sit together in the living room because that is the room whose purpose is to make this being together seem comfortable and natural. Even if we have some special activity in mind like a Bible study or home movies or a T-group, having it in the living room gives us the sense of being at home, which is where we would rather be than in some classroom or auditorium where the actual seating might be more efficiently arranged. To pursue these things in the setting of cushions, coffee, friends, and a fire is to transfigure them. We are putting the living room to the use it was designed for. For everything in it, no matter how splendid or how humble it is, how austere or how overstuffed, is assembled here with a double purpose: to give the illusion of our being at home (even in palaces there are soft cushions, reading lamps, and chairs facing each other), and to make that being at home actual.

For the living room is both a reality and a symbol. It is both itself and more than itself. Every piece of fabric speaks, and every pillow, lamp, table, plant, and picture. It may all say "cozy" or "elegant" or "comfy and bulgy" or "who cares," but all these statements are themselves variations on a single theme; namely, the decking of the life of the household in a way that reflects our feeling about it.

But I have been speaking of the living room as a place for entertaining. What about its plain day in and day out use by the family? What does it mean for them to be at home? Not that they must be gathered like some magazine-cover picture, all gingham and homespun and sampler, with granny in her rocker, mother with her basket, father with specs, book, and pipe, children sprawled all flannel-pajama'd on the hearth rug, and kitty batting a ball of yarn about. That picture has vanished into history along with foot-washing and boar's-head processions. But what about the remaining fact that our houses do have *living rooms* in them?

Is it not a picture in ordinary terms of what *families* are all about; namely, that these few people, thrust together and bound by the odd ties of flesh and blood, are given the chance to begin to learn the one big lesson that all men are given to learn—the lesson of Charity? That is, we were made for love, we are commanded to love, and since it doesn't come naturally to us, we have to learn to love. The family situation is, as it were, the elementary schoolroom where we start learning in small, easy, and natural ways to love—that is, to discover that self-giving, freedom, and joy are all one thing.

From the first coupling of the parents in desire for each other and for fruit, through the carrying of the first child by the mother and the husband's consideration for his pregnant wife, on through the suckling and feeding, to the training of the children ("Say 'thank you,'" or "Pick up your paper dolls," or "Stand up when your mother comes into the room,") and the ordinary muddle of things done together, it is all the school of Charity. For is not Charity the name given to that final, perfect, gloriously free and blissful state where all the lessons have been so mastered that the *rules* ("Pick up your paper dolls," or "Thou shalt not steal") have withered, and all of us have won through to the capacity to experience as joy the thing that was hinted at in all our early lessons; namely, that My Life For Yours *is* the principle at the bottom of everything, to embrace which is to live and to refuse which is to die? Heaven or hell.

This is carrying it high indeed—heaven and hell lurking in the living room. But if it is not this, what is it? What is "thank you" if it is not in its own modest way a form of the same thing which bursts gloriously upon us in the Apocalypse with "Worthy is the Lamb that was slain, and hast redeemed us to God by his blood"? If that seems a remote connection, think what both utterances mean. Do they not both mean "I owe this to you and I acknowledge it gratefully"? In the one case it may be a button sewed on or a door held open. In the other it is salvation. By getting accustomed to this simple, routine way of acknowledging our debts to each other, are we not thereby getting accustomed to what the City of God is like? Heaven is the place where these mutual acknowledgments are forms of joy; hell is the place where no such indebtedness is acknowledged at all.

Or again, an older brother showing his younger brother how to ride a bike or catch a football. What has that got to do with anything? Nothing much, really, unless we look at it for a moment. What is happening there? The older boy is offering something that he knows to the younger boy for the younger one's benefit. He is saying in effect, "Here. If you'll take what I have to offer, you will profit thus. Your experience will be enriched in this way." And the younger one, for his part, is saying, in effect, "I submit to you. You know something I don't. You be the boss here. I'm indebted to you."

Not that this high-sounding exchange is very likely to be articulated between the two lads, any more than we greet our guests in the hall with "Hail, noble lady," and so forth. There may be carping and grumbling attending the exercise, but it is nonetheless a case in point, in its own momentary way, of the biggest thing of all: My Life For Yours. Charity. If the older boy will not offer his knowledge, or if the younger one positively refuses all help, then the exchange breaks down in irritation and failure, and hell presumably is the place where irritation and failure rankle forever. Refusal, then, on the part of either boy would be a small lesson in hell, acceptance a small lesson in heaven. The one accepts the mantle of teacher momentarily; the other of pupil. The one gives something; the other receives.

It might be noted furthermore that in this kind of exchange of giving and receiving, the two are not cast in equal roles. Here they may learn what true hierarchy is all about; namely, the lovely rhythm of inequality as a mode of mutuality and joy. It is a state of affairs entirely repugnant to the imagination of hell, obsessed as that imagination is with questions of power, rights, and privilege. But questions of power, rights, and privilege have no meaning in this exchange here. The offering is real and free; the receiving is real and free. The authority of the teacher is assumed; the submission of the pupil is assumed. The success of the effort depends on the glad acceptance of this hierarchical ordering of things. The imagination of hell fears that somebody will think the teacher is better than the pupil. The imagination of Charity (that is, of heaven) can't see the problem: of course the teacher is better than the pupil, if you are talking about who knows how to ride the bike better; but if you are afraid that this means the pupil is somehow *worth* less than the teacher, you are into a paltry confusion. Snap out of it. If you try to even up the score by asserting the equal right of the pupil to express *his* views on how to keep the bike from wobbling into the nearest barberry hedge, then you will get exactly what you are setting up: chaos. A clamor of voices all insisting on equal dignity, equal time, equal influence, and equal rights, and nobody able to save the bike from collapsing or the boy from the prickles.

This is, to be sure, to wring a lot out of a small event. But if in such a small event we cannot see at work notions that obtain all up and down the ladder, then we are surely failing to call things by their names. Help is help, whether it is offered by a boy to his brother or by God to the world. Help, indebtedness, hierarchy, exchange, giving and receiving, My Life For Yours, joy—it is all there. You can find it in the little picture or the big one.

The lessons in Charity get harder though. We might hear in the living room some such exchange as this: "One piece of chocolate, Peter." "But I want some more." "No more." "Why?" "Because I said so." (And if Peter has not begun to learn his lessons, his next line is a screech. If he has learned them, it is "Yes, sir." And when he has learned them perfectly and has been set free at the far end of all his lessons, he himself will choose to stop at one chocolate.)

Surely here is one of the immensities in a nutshell, right here in one of the most ordinary of all household commonplaces. What is going on? Is it not Charity speaking with the voice of authority and severity and denial? And is that not a contradiction?

If we had no such commonplaces lying about and were left to speculate about Charity in a vacuum, we would most certainly think this was a contradiction. We would suppose that Charity was a lovely and soft thing, making us as comfortable and happy as possible at all times, and generally giving us what we want. It is obvious that that is how it works: if you love me, you'll want me to be happy. That's basic.

The trouble here is that we foreshorten the "you'll want me to be happy" part. Love does in fact want us to be happy and in order to bring us to that happiness, it does its best to steer us off bogus and destructive happinesses that promise instant fulfillment only to leave us wretched when the momentary happiness has run its course. "The chocolates taste so good: if one of them gives me this much pleasure, then two will give me twice as much. What could be more obvious? I will eat a dozen then." "No, Peter." "Why not? You're just being cruel. You don't like me. You want me to be unhappy. You like to see me suffer. You don't love me, you hate me."

How do we argue down this line of thought? It has all the evidence on its side. Chocolates *do* make me happy, and two chocolates *are* twice as good as one, and if you love me you must want me to be happy; therefore you will let me have these chocolates. It is absolutely unanswerable—and absolutely wrong.

How do we know it is wrong? Not because we

have unravelled all the high mysteries of the divine Love certainly. Rather, is it not because we are familiar with those mysteries from having had them set in our laps all along, so to speak? We have lived in families. We have been children and parents ourselves. The chocolates taste good, but they will make Peter vomit if he eats them all, and I love him and don't want him to vomit or become a sot; therefore I will forbid him this pleasure. From *his* point of view it is all too clear: I can't possibly love him, because I am making him unhappy. How shall I tell him that this cruelty on my part is boosting him directly on towards a freedom and power he can't even imagine right now—the freedom and power to desire and to choose authentic happiness? Left to his øwn way, he will choose the bogus, and land in surfeit and slavery (hell); led in mine, he will deny the bogus and choose the real, and find mastery and liberty (heaven). His way will lead him to the pestilent bog, mine to the glittering summit.

But of course we can't point all this out to him right on the spot when he is whining for the chocolates. We have to begin with "Because I said so." That is the first thing Peter must learn in the school of Charity. In this hierarchy of love, fathers are set over their sons—not because the fathers are better, or because they deserve this dignity, or any such thing, but because that is the part of the exchange they must supply for the time being. To the ears of the son, this is the first voice of authority, introducing the son to the fact that there is authority in the pattern and that not only is it possible to live with it and like it, but far beyond this, that this authority is the very fountainhead of his freedom and the guardian of his life. This is the way it is, and this is the way it has been since the beginning. Yahweh did not sit down at a round table with the patriarchs and say, "Here, let me sketch out the rationale for my plan for you and get some feedback from you on it." The prophets did not say, "Let's have some input from everyone and see what the consensus is." The apostles did not say, "Give us your insights, and we'll try to paste together some sort of evangel."

Sooner or later there is a *dictum* in this universe, and we men are indebted, nay we owe our life and salvation, to the fact that somebody said to us "Thus saith the Lord." That was not an invitation to a dialogue. It was the trumpet of authority, calling us to obedience and freedom and power and glory. The dialogue is a late arrival in human affairs, and hell may be the ultimate dialogue, twittering and droning forever and ever in a febrile caucus of input, insights, and feedback. Heaven is certainly the realm where authority, which we first encountered in the voice of our fathers, is hailed and praised as the rock of our liberty and joy.

But my "Because I said so" is, I say, an early

lesson that Peter must grasp. It is not the whole story, of course. When he has learned this first thing—that there is such a thing as authority and that it comes from the one who loves him—then he is beginning to move towards the place where he can understand what lies *behind* the "Because I said so," Then I will be able to say to him, "Come now and let us reason together." I can't say that at first—when he is reaching for the chocolates, say, or poking his infant finger towards the gas flame, or clambering over the window sill in the attic. "No!" is the saving utterance then. I would be guilty of sentimentalism and cynicism if, by dancing attendance on his baby whims, I betrayed him into the false set of expectations that attends the idea that love will do whatever he wants. Love will try to bring him to the thing he really wants after his desires and his will have been chastened, educated, and exercised to know what that thing is. When he is small, he doesn't know that there is a very great deal he doesn't know. Somehow he has to find this out, and the authority of his father (and mother, and teachers, and others) is a key to this discovery, since one of the biggest things he will eventually discover is that his real freedom is to be found, paradoxically, in obedience to the authority of the Most High. Hell is where they contest this forever. Heaven is where that obedience has been found to be synonymous with liberty and bliss. Desire and necessity have converged.

The parents and children, then, caught into the drama, are asked to bear their parts in the hierarchical exchanges of love.

But the living room. It is the place, we might say, which is hallowed by being full of this sense of mutuality and exchange. It is not built into the house for any specific activity as the kitchen or dining room or bedroom are. It is vaguely, or exactly rather, the place where everything else is gathered up and implicit. The family doesn't have to *do anything* special there. They may just *be* there, having set aside all the specific activities and sat down—comfortable, at home, at peace, relaxed, with the four walls defining the area in which their life together is to be carried on. They are acknowledging that this is "their" place, not in the sense of their barring everyone else, but of their taking up the responsibility for it, as a gardener his plot or a priest his shrine.

But, it may be remarked here, all this is fine, but it is not, surely, restricted to biological families, which seems to be part of your case here. Any group of people may take up living together, and may enact these rituals of domesticity that you are describing. Mutuality and giving and receiving and so forth ought to be put to work in any situation where two or ten or twenty people find themselves together. Why do you imply that Charity is recognized and enacted only in the biological family?

Most certainly, Charity is possible, nay, it is enjoined upon us, in all situations. In fact, it is much more clearly at work when the person I am put next to is not my flesh and blood brother. But that is exactly the point: flesh and blood furnish us with natural, and hence easy, *first* lessons in Charity. The ties that bind us to our father and mother and sisters and brothers take us several giant steps, so to speak, towards Charity. The loyalty and familiarity and fellowship that come along naturally with biological relationships ordinarily make the work of Charity much lighter. For instance, if someone cuts in ahead of me in a traffic jam and I am calling down plagues on his head and then see that he is my brother, somehow the curses die on my tongue. The job of forgiveness is suddenly easier. Or if we take a picnic to an isolated spot, going to great trouble to get away from crowds, only to find that another family has already spread itself out in the glade, we are full of resentment and hostility until we see that it is our sister and her children. The duty of generosity is suddenly easier. Or in an airplane, if I am hoping to have two seats to myself and then along comes a horrible person and plumps down, I feel petulant until I see that it is my son. The slight inconvenience of not being able to spread out suddenly evaporates.

The point here is that whatever the duties of

Charity are—of forgiveness, of generosity, of sharing, and so forth—we have them made easier for us by biology.

This is not to argue that nobody ever quarrels in families, or that Charity is never easy in extra-family situations (communes, orphanages, offices, etc.). It is simply to observe that we do in fact have, here at the obvious center of things, some built-in lessons in Charity, and that we are greatly helped in these lessons, in the usual run of things, by having our parents and brothers and sisters as teachers and classmates.

The fact that we get to calling intimate friends and trusted colleagues "brothers" and "sisters" witnesses to this, of course: we are trying to say that the intimacy and trust and love between us has come to the point where things seem to be as they are in biological families. I love you and you love me, and we share things and accept each other as brothers or sisters in the bigger family. And surely in good orphanages, say, where children have been denied this natural family, there will be earnest efforts to make the living conditions approximate family living as closely as possible—cottages and firesides and small groups gathered round an "aunt" or "uncle," rather than barracks and drills and vast hordes under the bark of a sergeant-major. A child brought up thus is being asked to live in a waterless waste.

But suppose all this is so. What is holy about the living room? Or rather, what is it about the whole enterprise that is celebrated as holy in this particular room?

Is it not that the bond that links these people together is understood to be a small case in point of what is true all up and down the ladder and finally in the City of God itself; namely, that the rule of love leads to joy, and that where that rule has broken down there is wrath and sorrow and frustration? In this family we can see exhibited all the joys and disciplines of love, naturally and daily, at work. If love rules, the enterprise succeeds: a happy household; heaven. Without love, the enterprise fails: a ruined household; hell. When these ordinary rhythms and exchanges of love are acknowledged, and when it is all lifted up in oblation to the Maker and Giver of it all, then the ordinariness becomes, like bread and wine, the very bearer of the heavenly immensities to us.

We might want to attach a postscript to these observations about the living room, since the case here has been that in this room we affirm, as it were, the idea of the family itself. This is an embattled idea in our own time, and the assault comes on three fronts: 1) the behavioral sciences have filled us all with suspicion and fear about family relationships—our mothers are dominant, our fathers are villains, we are eaten up with sibling rivalry, etc; 2) traditional family bonds are hated and scorned by the armies that march under the general banner of "liberation," the idea here being that to be shut into this sexually-determined scheme of things is to be a prisoner; 3) we see before our eyes the evidence of chaos in the break-up of approximately one in two families.

We shall have to decide just what it is that we do think about this business of finding ourselves in families. To help us, we have the voice of history, myth, tradition, and Scripture in one ear, and of contemporaneity in the other.

6

The dining room is set apart for an activity that can occur elsewhere. Mere eating is a simple enough affair to be done in the kitchen or the living room. So if there is a room which can be stricken from the blueprint in the interest of economy or efficiency, it is the dining room. Many houses and apartments are built with dining ells or dining areas, and of course caves, wigwams, and cottages never had much in the way of dining rooms. But whether it is a room or not, the space designated for eating is something we will find in any dwelling ever conceived for human habitation. And we may find dining *rooms* in houses where there is enough space to allow this mere eating to appear in all of its appropriate dignity.

Dignity? Eating? Never. Eating is the most undignified of things, what with chewing and swallowing and enzymes and gas and one thing and another. Any dignity that we invest it with is an illusion we work up to hide from ourselves these embarrassing reminders of the mortality which we share with pigs and worms. Come.

That is a brisk view, but it will not quite do. To believe it is to reject the most obvious thing in all of human experience; namely, that eating is a ceremonial activity. Every place mat we ever set out, every fork we put to the left of a plate, every arrangement of food on a platter sings this out clearly to us. It is not just a question of formal dinners in the dining room either. When we eat in the kitchen, which most of us do most of the time, we still set the stage carefully, again with fork to the left, knife to the right, napkin here, glass there, and so on. There is clearly much more at stake here than the mere function of transferring nourishment from outside our bodies to inside. This could be done with pills or liquids or needles, or mash heaped in a trough. But somehow these clinical and barnyard arrangements do not appeal to us.

Why don't they appeal to us? They are certainly more efficient and probably cheaper than what we do. What is going on in our imagination that makes us go to all this trouble to deck and festoon this thrice-daily necessity?

In the first place, we are the sort of creatures who have ceremonialized nearly everything we do. We may miss this in an epoch like ours, which is in hot pursuit of the "unstructured" and the spontaneous and the *ad hoc*. We may tend to think of highly-structured and ceremonialized things as fake. To get towards authenticity, we are told, we need to dismantle things and let our hair down. Expressions popular in the last decade or so attest to this: "*Do* it!" or "Let it all hang out!" The words "conventional" and "traditional" are words that arouse suspicion in us, the idea being that they are more or less synonymous with "repressive." And so we try earnestly to be "innovative" and "creative."

But we may have been fooled. We may be like Daedalus and Icarus trying to fly, or the rabbit who wanted red wings; that is, we may be trying to do something we can't quite do when we try to "de-ceremonialize" everything. Our distrust of structures and conventions may betray a touching naivete on our part. Perhaps for all of our zeal in the pursuit of spontaneity and innovation, we are missing the stark truth about what we are: highly ceremonial, even ritual, creatures who move at the tag end of a millennia-long procession of humanity who have all ceremonialized things. The ancients were not necessarily more stupid than we are: indeed, there is some reason for supposing that they may from time to time have seen things more clearly than we do.

If this is so, then a wise generation will take its cues from its elders and teachers—its forerunners, in other words. There will be no question of jettisoning all that has gone before, any more than there is of an architect's throwing out the principles by which older builders held up the roof of the Parthenon or Chartres.

In other words, there are some things that are always there. We can't float the Astrodome on nothing, or hang the roof of the Kennedy Center on a skyhook. One way or another, we take our cues from our predecessors and follow in the way they have beaten for us. If this humbling observation does not appeal to us, we may of course wipe the slate clean and start from scratch. But one fine day we will find we have "discovered" exactly what they were telling us all along.

The argument of this book is that this is true morally as well as architecturally. There are some things that are *there*, whether they happen to appeal to us or not—things like the Ten Commandments or family structures. We are busy dismantling most of them right now. But the archaeologists of A.D. 4000 will ferret devoutly, trying to piece together just why it was that this century thought it could do that.

One of the things that is there is ceremony. Ritual. This decking of ordinary functions so that they become occasions. We do it with all of the events that matter to us: birth, victory, marriage, achievement, death, and so forth. Every cake, every palm, every veil and bouquet and limousine, every scroll of parchment, and every cortege is a waste of time and money if it is true that we are better off having things unstructured and unritualized, since that is what all of these things involve. It is hard indeed to argue down the unstructuralists: they can appeal to common sense and efficiency. They have all the obvious trumps—except for the past and the future, which they reject. To the man who says, "Down with all this complicated structure and ritual; let's have honesty and simplicity and efficiency," we can only ask, "Were *all* the ages before us out of their minds?" and again, "Tell us, then, about the forms of beauty and dignity and joy that your new efficiency will open up to us." These two questions would want answering.

But we ceremonialize, or ritualize, the ordinary things as well as the special occasions. Eating food is the most ordinary of all things, and it is embarrassingly functional. Biology and anatomy can account for the whole process for us, except that we don't want to leave it at biology and anatomy. We

64

don't want to be thinking of tubes and bladders and capillaries when we sit down to our wedding feast or even to our Thursday breakfast. We want things orderly and attractive—structure and ceremony, in other words. But is it all illusion and fastidiousness, all this festooning of the process—this putting out of napkins and cutting the toast on the diagonal? Would we be freer men if we simplified the whole process, and thought of eating mainly in purely functional terms? Perhaps we ought to approach our mealtimes talking gaily of our esophagi and our colons.

One view would say yes. The view being put here says no. It says that really free men see and acknowledge what all poets and most philosophers have seen; namely, that the commonplace things are both themselves and more than themselves, and that in order to perceive this "more than," we have to festoon things.

For instance, your best beloved is, to be sure, a mere assemblage of tissue and lymph and so forth; but she is also an image of the Divine Beauty, and you know that you are speaking more accurately about her when you reach for the vocabulary of roses, lilies, angels, and goddesses than the vocabulary of the clinic. Or again, bread may be a plain white sandwich loaf or Ritz crackers, but it is also an image of the flesh of the Incarnate God; and in order to perceive this latter clearly, we deck it with the vocabulary of mystery, altar, and eucharist, not the vocabulary of the bakery. But the bread is no *less* a bakery product when it is on the Lord's Table than when it is in the oven: indeed, there is a sense in which it is only on that Table that we see clearly what all bakeries are really about.

Which brings us back around to the dining room. This room says, in effect, that the common, daily, necessary business of eating is just that—common, daily, and necessary—but that it is also a picture of the thing that lies at the root of all life; namely, the principle of exchange. My Life For Yours. We enact that principle whenever we assemble and sit down at the table. We may be sitting down to cornflakes, pizza, or Beluga caviar, but whatever it is, life has been laid down for us. We are receiving life by chewing and swallowing the life of something else. We have to do it to stay alive. We have to do it daily. As long as we live, we will be doing it. Nothing could be more ordinary and functional. But there it is—the biggest mystery of all, right there before us, three times a day. We are enacting the rite. We are participating in the holy mystery.

The idea that ordinariness should be thus fraught with heaven, and that a thing like mere eating should open out onto vistas that we thought were the province of religious mystery—it is all too heady. Not that we are transported every time we sit down to our cornflakes, any more than we are struck with Cupid's dart every time we come across our spouse. But the thing which from time to time we *are* given to see when our vision is roused—that eating *is* a mysterious thing, or that our spouse *is* fairer than Aphrodite—it is there all along, cloaked in the demure mantle of ordinariness. It is only now and again that we are vouchsafed a clear vision of it. In the ordinary run of things, we live with it, and affirm it if we ever think of it, and draw our life from it. My spouse really is most fair: but it is only the awakened vision of love that sees all of her splendor. This food really is exchanged life; but it is only in the eucharistic vision that this becomes apparent.

What is this "eucharistic vision" that is supposed to be at work over our cereal? Is it not simply the setting into focus of what we see in a blur all the time anyway; namely, that we have no life except what we owe to the laying down of some other life, and hence that thanksgiving is the appropriate response? The eating of food is seen not so much as the gobbling of what is my due, as the receiving of a most holy benefit. Holy because whether the ox in the stockyards knew it or not as he was being hit on the head, or the kernel of corn as it was being pulverized in the mill, this is death in order that someone else (me) might live. It may be involuntary for this ox or this kernel, but the thing is at work nonetheless. And not only Jews and Christians, but all men everywhere (until we sailed out into modernity) have known that this is a holy business. Life laid down so that other life may spring forth. Life from death. The most sacred mysteries, shrouded behind smoke and veils and portals, and laid out there in your cereal bowl.

If this commonplace of daily life bears this sort of freight, then we do well to deck it. Candles for birthdays, bouquets for weddings, parchment for graduations—and the table set for breakfast.

And, if a house happens to have a dining room, the idea at work in that room is that there are times (the evening meal every night? special occasions? all three daily meals?) when it is appropriate to mark the business of eating by setting it entirely apart from all the other functions of the household, and to approach it as the occasion when men and women and children may enact together their common humanness, that is, their mutual indebtedness to the principle of exchanged life. Sometimes, on a specially festive occasion, the question of mere nourishment is almost wholly transfigured in the rite: now we are thinking, not of filling our stomachs, but rather of fellowship. We invite you. We welcome you. We sit down at the table with you. We break bread with you. To be sure, there is a biological need being met here, but the meeting of that need is not now foremost in our minds: it has been caught up and made the vehicle of a great and splendid thing—fellowship.

Again, any Jew, any Christian, and any religious pagan is already familiar with this threefold trans- action in which food is taken (flesh or bread or wine, say), and then offered up, and then eaten. The sacred banquet. Not just an altar but a table: or perhaps rather, not just a table but an altar. Which way is it? This sitting down around this table with our family or with our guests is an act in which we may perceive and mark and celebrate the thing which is true: that our fellowship with each other is most literally a matter of eating together, since it is here that we not only profess, but also enact, our common indebtedness to the order of exchanged life. As you and I break this bread together, we signal and enact together our participation in the order of creation (we both depend on bread to stay alive), and we seal our solidarity with each other (this bread broken between us will become the sign of the love that will obtain between you and me: my life laid down for you; my life drawn from yours laid down for me). For Christians, of course, the whole thing is caught up in the biggest transaction of all, of which all these smaller transactions are but examples, namely, the life of the Lamb of God laid down so that we might live.

Besides these eucharistic mysteries at work in our ordinary eating and drinking, we may see in the dining room, as we saw in the hall, the question of appropriateness at work. Just as the lawn mower in the hall seemed inappropriate to the general idea of front halls, so the laundry basket, say, on the sideboard in the dining room seems to fit ill. Why?

Because the idea at work in sideboards is something like this: here is a piece of furniture whose job is to hold things—linen, silverware, china—that belong to dining. Now dining is a noble business, with men and women made in the image of God facing each other around a table and breaking bread together. This comes pretty close to the heart of things. Seeing that it is this kind of activity engaged in by this kind of creature, it is perhaps appropriate to deck it carefully and beautifully at times. The silver and linen and china are a sort of costly offering brought to the occasion, as men have always brought offerings that cost them something to their holy places. (Not that we must have Tiffany and Spode: we may have earthenware dishes, made with our own hands; or Woolworth plastic which, if it is set forth with candor and love, becomes gold and silver.) And if the dishes and flatware are themselves ennobled by being the vessels and utensils used in this solemnity, then we don't want them dumped in a bin or scattered about on counter tops with the milk cartons and ketchup bottles—not, in any case, if we are interested in keeping alive in our household the sense of the dignity that attends ordinariness, and hence of the appropriateness of making distinctions between one function (preparing the food—the milk cartons, etc.) and another (eating the food—the dishes and cutlery). Let us house these vessels and utensils in something beautiful—something that answers in its material and design and craftsmanship to these noble vessels. Hence let us find fine wood, and let us expend time and skill on designing a noble housing. It is appropriate. It echoes the music of the rite itself, we might say, rather than setting up some alternative clangor.

Whereas the laundry, on the other hand, does set up an alternative clangor. It is a discord in this harmony. To be sure, the pieces in the basket may be most beautiful (a blouse from Bonwit; a shirt from Turnbull Asser) or necessary (underpants). But they do not fit in this part of the rite, any more than the fatty parts of the lamb were brought to the altar of incense in the Tabernacle. Fatty parts here; incense over here. Divide up the items necessary to the rite into their appropriate distinctions for their special tasks. No slur on any of them is implied. It is just that in order to celebrate the whole rite, you have to do one thing here and another here and not run it all together. The laundry bespeaks a different part of the rite: necessary, good, and holy, but different. Don't put (or at least don't *leave*) the laundry basket on the sideboard.

There is one other thing about the dining room that may be worth noting. It is the question of seating arrangement. When we have guests there is a certain amount of mulling on the part of the hostess as to who shall sit where. There is the merely psychological angle to this problem, of course: who will keep this person happy? who will be able to cope with this harpy? whom shall we put next to Mrs. Entwistle? But there is also the more elusive and delicate business of honor. There has traditionally been a pecking order, and it is still to some extent observed in houses where guests are entertained at table. It doesn't have to be observed, of course, and if the note we want to strike at a given entertainment is mere *bonhomie*, then there is something to be said for letting everyone scramble for chairs. But if we do care to observe the convention of seating arrangement, then we are into a purely ceremonial, or ritual, question, since obviously where we sit does not affect the intake of food.

And it is not only when we are giving a formal entertainment that this question arises. In ordinary household routine there has commonly been the idea of having the father sit at the "head" of the table (this becomes a problem at round tables—a problem which King Arthur recognized and turned to good purpose). The idea was a patriarchal one since in Jewish and Christian households, the father was thought to be somehow ultimately responsible for bearing the burden of authority in the house. This idea is assailed by the people who see it as unfair to the "rights" of the rest of the family, but that is not how the tradition understood it. The idea was that here, as with the case of the father asserting his authority over his son, say, we find the father bowing to the role, or task, that he has been given in the design of things. ("Roles" are interchangeable at random to modern thought: Jews and Christians, on the other hand, have thought they were anchored into the Creation somehow.) The father's burden was that he was answerable to heaven for the household. With this awesome responsibility went the "leadership," symbolized by such common tokens as his sitting at the head of the table. It was simply a way of displaying in a small, visible, daily convention what was true.

The convention is doubtless unacceptable to modern thought since it smacks of patriarchy. We are free to realign our seating conventions at our tables to bring them into harmony with contemporaneity, but there will be some Jews and some Christians who will suspect that the tradition has roots in something more ancient than a power grab by the men. In any event, my general point about dining rooms as the locale for one important part of the rite celebrated in well-ordered households does not stand or fall thereby. It may be noted in passing that contemporary imagination concerns itself with the order of power, and hence must speak politically, asserting people's rights and so forth, as though the household is a small state. The traditional Jewish and Christian imagination concerned itself with the order of love and hence could talk of hierarchy or patriarchy without anyone's becoming alarmed.

7

The kitchen is not one of the front rooms usually. Is this because we are ashamed of what goes on there, and don't want to admit to each other, much less to outsiders, that food has to be prepared and things washed up, and that there are heat and grease and orange peels and coffee grounds and soapy water behind the scenes? Wouldn't we do better to make the kitchen one of the front rooms? It is certainly at the center of activity in any household. We might honor it by making it the first thing inside the front door.

There are places, of course, where you do come upon the cooking and washing up straight off. All wigwams and all cottages in fairy tales have the cooking going on right there in front of you when you come in. The squaw poking at the venison savoury or the goodwife with her loaves all crusty on the brick hearth—these are what you encounter here. Isn't this a good scheme? It is simple and homey and candid, as though to say, "When you come in here you are welcomed into the very bosom of the life here. We do not keep you sitting stiffly on a plush chair in the hall. Welcome to the inner circle."

This is appealing, and it is one way of doing things. What, then, is the idea at work in the other way—having the kitchen "behind the scenes," as it were?

Does it not have something to do with the human sense that getting food ready and cleaning up afterwards are jobs that don't especially need to be displayed? We can, of course, display the art of cooking if we want to. Indeed, it makes for a popular sort of television program. But when we do display cooking, it is usually in order to teach something, or to let everybody have a peek at how it's done. Here is how you use the shears to cut up this lobster; here is how to scald milk; here is how to punch down dough. But the general idea in preparing food (or preparing anything at all for that matter) is to get it ready *for* something. The baking is *for* the table, not vice versa. Peeling potatoes and dicing carrots and slicing onions are only to fix them *for* the goulash. Even when we get to *cordon bleu* cuisine, with whole salmon all be-jellied and be-truffled, and cornish game hens all luxurious in beds of chestnut puree—even here the preparation is not the *point*. The main point is to make the business of eating splendid: to deck it appropriately for the festive occasion, as though to say, Look, food itself is full of glory; see how it comes to the feast garnished and piquant, as you come to the feast dressed and groomed. The chef wants us to think about his finished product, and to have our palates roused in anticipation of eating these dainties. If we are thinking primarily about the knives and saucepans and whisks that he used, then he has failed; just as you have failed if, when you arrive at the banquet with your complexion all petal-like, we think primarily of the pads and bottles and unguents in your boudoir that stand behind this achievement. The preparation is *for* the occasion. When the occasion begins, the work of preparing things is put out of sight.

Similarly, the cleaning and washing up in the kitchen after meals is not the thing itself. It looks back to the meal just finished, and it looks forward to the meals to come. We need to get the gravy off these plates so we can put our eggs on them tomorrow morning. On one accounting then, everything that goes on in the kitchen is nothing in itself. It is just a perennial getting ready and cleaning up. It looks ahead to the activity, which is the sitting down to eat.

It is, in other words, service. All service is like this. It is all a matter of getting things ready for something, or of cleaning them up afterwards. If we want to speak of the laundry and the broom closet together with the kitchen, we can see the same thing. Service. Clothes are made to be worn and seen, not washed. That is, they are not made for the sake of the washing machines. If they are washable, this is a convenience secondary to their first function which is to appear on us. Washing is nothing in itself: it merely looks back to the time(s) we have worn the socks and forward to the times we will want to wear them again. The socks are simply *going through* the wash so that they can get back to doing the thing they were made to do; namely, adorn our ankles. Similarly with the mops and rags: they do not hang next to the sofa or the sideboard, since their particular function is to keep the living room or the dining room ready for whatever goes on there. We can include the tool-shed here as well: we do not ordinarily display tacks, friction tape, and drills on the mantel or on an end table. Is this because they are ignoble, or worth less than the gewgaws that do get displayed on mantels and end tables? Is it not rather that service, represented by washing machines and mops and drills, is most truly itself when it is *happening?* Its whole reason for being is to prepare something *else*, not to parade itself. Service exists only in the doing, and all its paraphernalia lies ready for it between times—not, like the damask on the walls or the tureen on the table, to be seen and hailed for itself, but rather to wait in obscurity for the next job. (A poet or seer might press this line of thought far enough to see analogies even in the human body, where the plumbing and wiring are generally concealed.)

We begin to get anxious at a string of observations like this, though, since it looks as if it is heading pell-mell towards a case for slavery or elitism (if the paraphernalia is hidden and humble, let's keep the people who do the work hidden and humble). And if we were speaking politically, this would be a highly dangerous line of thought, leading swiftly to a warrant for all sorts of tyranny and privilege and oppression. For politics has to try to get as close to justice as possible without counting on charity, and therefore it must rely on a delicate and explosive weighing and balancing of everybody's rights against everybody else's. It is a more or less impossible job, as the agony and frustration of all political schemes attest, and we do the best we can with democracy.

But a more radical order of things is supposed to be at work in households. Here the idea is that in our daily routines we are playing out the Drama of

Charity, which eludes politics and its calculations. The commonplaces of household life are parts of the rite in which we celebrate the mystery of Charity—and it is indeed a mystery, full of outrageous absurdities like obedience being a form of liberty, and self-denial a form of self-discovery, and giving a form of receiving, and service a form of exaltation. Politics boggles at mysteries like this; but in Christian households the hunch is that they are all clues to what the Real Drama is about.

For when the Drama of Charity was played out on the stage of our history, we saw these absurdities disclosed in their true colors. Here we saw Love incarnate in the form of a servant; here we heard the disquieting doctrine of exchanged life proclaimed all over the hills of Judaea; here we witnessed the humility of the virgin mother exalted high above the station of patriarchs and prophets, and the heroic silence of her spouse lauded for all time. Here we saw a gibbet transfigured into a throne, defeat into victory, death into life, and submission into sovereignty. And here we learned of the Holy Ghost himself whose service is to glorify, not himself, dread and mighty as he is, but this incarnate Love humbled below the meanest of men. A riot of self-giving and glory, humiliation and exaltation, service and majesty. Nonsense by any political calculating; but the mystery of Charity before our eyes.

It is this nonsense that we come upon in our kitchens. For the service in this room is either pointless thralldom, or it is as close to the center of the Real Drama as any rite in the whole household. For it is, precisely, service; and service, occurring as it does always for the sake of something else, is a form of humility and self-giving; and humility and self-giving have been disclosed in the Christian Drama as being at the heart of the matter.

If this is true, then it may be that we men generally get things backwards. For ordinarily we fancy that power and glory are the important things, and hence we all naturally hanker to have a place where the power and glory are. Caesar in his triumphal car with all of Rome at his feet; Charlemagne crowned by the Pope on Christmas Day; the President mounting the rostrum to the sound of "Ruffles and Flourishes"—this is where the Real Things are, and the rest of us live somewhere down the line from there. This, we must admit, is what arises naturally in our imaginations.

But if we think, as Christians do, that Love is at the center, then we have got to reconsider. Obviously the triumphs and pomps and accolades are themselves in the service of something greater than they are: it is their office to do service to the man who has done service to the kingdom. Caesar is doing his work when he is up in Gaul carrying out the work of the Empire, and that is hard work indeed, asking every ounce of his intelligence, courage, and endurance (the question as to whether we agree that he should have been there to begin with does not affect the point that is being made here). The procession in Rome is a response to his service. It is not his daily routine to ride in chariots through arches. By the same token, Charlemagne's work in life is not to kneel perpetually at the presbytery steps while the Supreme Pontiff in gold mitre and cope raises the crown over his head. His work is to serve the Frankish Empire by seeing that justice and peace prevail, and that is hard work indeed. Or again, the President is not elected to mount rostrums while music plays: his service is back in the Oval Office with his counsellors, toiling through briefs and trying to make decisions that affect history. A heavy burden.

But of course there is something waggish about a line of thought like this. It is as though we are working up to saying, "See? Your service at the dishpan is the real thing. Those imperial splendors are worth less than your chapped hands." The only response most of us could give to that line would be, "Well fine. I'll be happy enough to settle for the second best, the imperial splendors. Bring them on."

We are bedazzled, in other words, by the appeal of power and glory, and it is nearly impossible for us to keep our imaginations steady in their grasp of the Real Thing that lies just below the surface of all our ordinariness; namely, that this ordinariness, with all that it involves of tedium and service and obscurity, is the vehicle given to us by which we may move towards the power and glory we dream of—a power and glory spoken of more accurately, we might remember, in the story of the Virgin than in the story of Caesar.

So that the kitchen is one room in the house where we may see enacted this much of the rite. Preparing food for the table and cleaning up afterwards are, like the tasks of the Virgin and Joseph and Christ and the Holy Ghost in the Drama of Charity, obscure and menial. To the eye of Pontius Pilate (politics, that is), it must have all looked egregiously dull. But some people think there was more than meniality and dullness there. They think it is a drama about love, and hence about majesty and liberty and hilarity. But of course they cannot convince Pilate of this. He would think that *all* tasks like this—the man shackled to his plow, his spear, or his desk, trying to win food for the table; or the woman bound to her oven, her bowl, or her dish-pan, trying to prepare and clean up that food—are just part of the treadmill that the masses are doomed to tread and thank goodness he has servants to do this for him.

We come here upon one of the paradoxes in the drama. Work (e.g., plowing or cooking) was laid on us in our exile from Eden, along with our clothes. At that point we lost the noble capacity to experience our routine responsibilities as a joyous dance, as Adam and Eve had presumably experienced them in Eden. Work became, precisely, drudgery. For most of us it is a lifelong matter of doing tasks that are more or less menial and more or less dull. Some people, of course, escape this: very rich people, or very brilliant people, or very influential people; or the few, like oceanographers or wildlife photographers or crime reporters or fashion designers, who have fascinating jobs. But for most of us, the daily task is a pretty repetitious matter.

But this plain work, which is part of our exile, is, paradoxically, our salvation, on at least two levels. First, of course, it saves us from sheer leisure, which is a terrible state of affairs, bringing with it ennui, surfeit, irritation, and restlessness. We need only to look at the life-style of the idle rich, or the ways in which leisured civilizations amuse themselves, or the trivialities that eat up the time in retirement centers to see that this is so. Much as we dream of prolonged leisure, we find that it stultifies us when we get it. The first part of the paradox, then, is that our "punishment" is also a defense for us, just as our clothes are.

But our work is our salvation in more than just this negative sense of protecting us from mere leisure. It is also our service to each other and to the

Most High. For it is in our work, as well as in our relationships, that we may begin to experience what Charity is all about.

Looked at professionally or economically, of course, most work is drudgery, and we have to ginger it up with coffee breaks, Muzak, fringe benefits, and psychiatric help. And this is all necessary and right, for just as politics has to protect us with secondary measures like equal rights because it cannot count on our loving each other, so businesses have to come to our rescue because we are not working for love.

But in households we have the chance to experience and celebrate work for what it really and truly is: a form of service, that is, of love offered to others. The question of payment and rights recedes somehow. The mother suckling her infant in the middle of the night does not call up her lawyer to see what can be done about suing the baby for infringement of her right to sleep. The father at his plow or his desk does not keep a tally of hours and then calculate to see whether his wife is putting in as many as he. When there is luggage to be carried, we don't distribute the weight equally among the men and the women in the family. And so forth.

But of course it's not *fair* for the father to push the wretched plow decade after decade. And it's not fair for the mother to have to suckle *all* the babies in the family and knead all the dough. Politically, it is outrage and what we need is revolution to overturn this tyrannous order of things!

And the people in a household where love is at work look at us blankly, unable to grasp what we are raging about. They know nothing of this kind of calculated equality and fairness. They assumed that they were doing simply what they had been given to do, and if they thought about it at all, they would have chalked it all up to duty, or love, or . . . And they would have had trouble defining which it was. For in the order of Charity, which is what households are about, the duties of love and the love of duty are indistinguishable.

Not, of course, that everyone goes skipping and whistling about his tasks. The father is not obliged to caper along behind his plow, any more than the mother is called upon to be singing canticles of bliss over the suds all day long. The hour after hour, year after year routine is no doubt unexciting; and more often than not, this "love" of duty takes the form of simply doing it because it is the next thing, exactly as our "love" of our spouse often takes the form of simply doing the thing because that is what Charity does (the glass of water in the middle of the night; the helping hand with the dishes or the flat tire). Nobody supposes for a moment that it is all ecstatic. Learning to love is like learning anything else: a great deal of it is a matter of fumbling through the steps until they become automatic and habitual. The saints would tell us that their freedom and joy stand at the far end of long years of getting into habits of Charity. It is not all ecstatic. The household duties of love are very much like our human existence itself: glorious and sparkling when you think of the big things—Creation and Resurrection and the Vision of God; but handed to us from hour to hour, year to year, in muted, plain forms.

Which is the whole point about kitchens, and about households, and about families, and about ordinariness itself. The splendid mysteries are there, acknowledged and celebrated in common-place routines. The supposition at work all the time is that these routines are like the tips of icebergs, say, or peepholes through which we may glimpse huge vistas of joy. The man following the plow along thousands of miles of furrow year after year or sitting in endless committee meetings, or the woman cooking ten thousand meals and washing a hundred thousand dishes, and both of them doing it, really, for the sake of each other and for their children—are these not cases in point of the vast thing that Charity is about; namely, exchanged life? My Life For Yours? And do Christians not believe that, fully revealed, this Charity will turn out to be ecstatic, hilarious, and splendid beyond imagining? Otherwise, what is all the imagery of heaven about? It is either a lot of whistling in the dark, an opiate concocted by the worst sort of wizard to keep us meekly at our plows and our stoves (as Marx and the lib people will have it), or it is True.

It is easy enough to see how a feudal or capitalistic mind can take this line of thought and manipulate it to justify sweat shops, child labor, and slavery. Just keep at your humble work there, all you drabs, tots, and serfs: glory is waiting. That is a cynical counterfeit of the truth, as rape is the counterfeit of true sexuality, gluttony the counterfeit of true eating, or plunder of true exchange. Every good thing has its counterfeit.

The good thing that sets a household apart from sweat shops, child labor, and slavery is, precisely, love. Charity. There is no other way around it. The father *is* the slave to his plow or his desk; the mother *is* a slave to her stove or her tub—unless there is another factor at work which completely escapes political tallying. Only that father or that mother can tell you how it is that their work has been transfigured. If the father had any sense, he would abandon all this ballast of spouse and children and use his money for himself. If the mother had any sense, she would throw this truculent and demanding infant straight out the window.

But somehow there is an alchemy at work in households which transmutes the lead of duty and drudgery into gold. It is the alchemy of love, and where it is not working properly we get lead again. The father is restless and irritated; the mother is bored and afflicted. Neither is considering the other, supporting the other, relieving the other, helping the other. Ennui, disenchantment, frustration—hell, in a word.

The solution often suggested for this unhappy situation (which is more and more widespread in our own time because we are a politically-minded people) is that we "restructure" everything. Equalize the tasks; keep a tally; even up the scores; shuffle the roles. And if all else fails, have a creative divorce.

While granting that divorce, like an aspirin or an enema, may be the only thing left for a bad situation, Jews and Christians would have difficulty with the general suggestion here, since it assumes that we can come at a mystery with a computer. The computer can, of course, tell us who worked at which task for how many hours yesterday, and therefore whose turn it is today. But it cannot tell us why a man should leave his father and mother and cleave to his wife, nor why that man should push that plow year after year, nor why his wife should stagger about for nine months every couple of years bearing the fruit of his momentary pleasure, nor why she should get up a hundred nights in a row to suckle his infant and hers; nor why this ridiculous treadmill is spoken of in a holy Book as being a picture of the mystery of Christ and the Church.

The computer and its programmers will smell a plot and set about to rip it all up. They will demolish the sanctuary and tear down the veils that hide the holy things. But there will be some people who will want to get on with the rite on the belief that it does in fact have something to do with self-giving, which has something to do with Charity, which has something to do with Joy.

The kitchen is one of the rooms where we may start learning the rite.

8

The idea of a chapter on the bathroom might make us anxious. Must we be led into a myopic scrutiny of everything that goes on in *there*? Will we be obliged to wring significance from all this porcelain? Oh dear.

"Oh dear" is probably as just a reaction as any. It is not only the Victorians who closed the door on this set of activities. We would have to search far and wide for a tribe or a civilization anywhere that did not go behind doors or around a bush or outside the wall for what we shut up in our bathrooms. Is it because everyone has always been ashamed of sheer bodily necessity? Are we embarrassed by the most natural things of all? That surely can't be healthy?

And on first glimpse it isn't. There must be some massive breakdown in our handling of experience for us all to pretend all the time that this whole class of activities doesn't exist (for is that not what we are saying, with our closed doors and the taboos we put on polite talk?). Wouldn't it be much more realistic if we burst open these doors and bundled our tubs and toilets out into the center of things? Come, let's be honest and natural, for until we are we will never be free.

This sounds bracing, but it may be worth our asking why the tradition of concealing things arose. Outside the wall, or behind bushes or closed doors: why have men done it that way? Is it unhealthy shame?

Unhealthy no. Shame yes.

Shame is not necessarily unhealthy. It may be a matter of wanting to veil what ought to be veiled. It may not be so much a matter of our being mortified at having been caught at something we never should have been doing as of our saying it would be a shame to parade something that ought not to be paraded. Shame, in other words (and with it closed doors), may be an index of how seriously we take the notion of the private. Do we grant that there are in fact some things that ought to be veiled? Put another way, does everyone have a warrant to see everything?

There is one ferociously hearty view that would say yes, everyone does have such a warrant, and there is nothing that may be veiled. What's mine is thine, and what's thine is mine, so let's get it all out in the open. Politically, this view takes the form of a radical communalism in which all private property is abolished, all fences torn down, and all memberships dissolved, since all discrimination is thought to be evil. No one may be barred from any association, any privilege, any garden, on any basis whatever. "The people" own everything and have a right to everything. Psychologically, this bristling public-spiritedness takes the form of T-groups, "sharing," and other forms of emotional rape in which the idea is that I have a right to know all the deepest secrets of your psyche even though you and I have only just met. If it's hidden, it's unhealthy. Morally, this viewpoint produces pornography, open marriage, and "frankness," the idea being again that the only way to have things natural and free is to break down the doors of censorship, fidelity, and reticence.

On the other hand, there is the idea that some things ought to be veiled, and that everyone does not have a warrant to go in everywhere and watch everything. We can see this idea at work in every closed door, every veil, every taboo, and every "thou shalt not" in history and myth. There is always something that I am not allowed to see or touch, or somewhere I am not allowed to go. The virgin goddess Diana wears a tunic because I am not allowed to see her nakedness, and woe to Actaeon who watched her bathing. The Ark of the Covenant has golden rings and carrying poles so that not even the Levites have to touch its burning sanctity, and woe to Uzzah who put out his hand to steady it. The privy council of the khan, the chairman, or the president meets behind locked doors, and woe to the interloper.

In all of these there is visible the idea that distinctions have to be made, in this case not simply neutral distinctions such as those we make between blue and red, say, or hot and cold, but between who may and who mayn't. This is full-dress discrimination: some of us are *left out*. We are being discriminated against because we haven't got the right credentials. I, for example, am a man and married, and am thereby disqualified from being one of Diana's maidens, and they are the only ones who may see her naked. I am neither a Jew nor a priest, much less a high priest, so I am barred from approaching the Ark. I am not privy to the president's counsel, so I can't go in there. Veils, taboos, closed doors everywhere I turn.

And the door to the bathroom is closed too. What is that all about? Come, I know what you're doing in there and I know what you look like and furthermore I do it myself frequently. Open up.

But no. Not that anything calamitous would happen if I did blunder in, mind you. I would probably not be changed into a stag like Actaeon, or struck dead like Uzzah, or hanged like the interloper. There would be a brief flurry, with the shower curtain being whisked around or a towel flapped, and me back out in the hall red-faced.

Why this hugger-mugger in ordinary household routines?

Is it not that even here, far from the veils and smoke and mystery of religious sanctuaries, we still acknowledge the validity of privacy as a sort of guardian of things that should be private? We mortals suspect that we have to distinguish sharply between the clothed self that we present to others and our naked self. No one knows, of course, just exactly where the frontier is between what is safe and what is perilous. Locker rooms with a hundred naked bodies are generally held to be fair enough; and undressing for the doctor, while it is a bore, seems to be warranted; and public "facilities" have only the sketchiest of token barriers between the stalls. But that there is such a frontier very few tribes and civilizations have doubted.

If someone trots out the idea of naked tribes with their unspoiled freedom and unembarrassed openness, two comments might be ventured. First, be they never so bare, there are conventions of modesty among the most starkly naked people that no one may violate with impunity. Second, we may ask whether their nakedness is a model to be held up to civilized men: the "noble savage" is a creature found mainly in the poetry of romantic nostalgia for Eden and in the painting of Gauguin.

And Eden itself deserves a comment here, since it is often a sort of back-to-Eden wish that lies behind the promise that we shall return to innocence by taking off our clothes and being natural and simple and free. The trouble with this is that we are not in Eden any more. The whole point of that story is that we are exiles. We aren't at home, alas. We hope we may find our way back there, or better yet (says the Christian idea) on to the paradise of which Eden itself was only a shadow. But in the meantime, we have lost that lovely naturalness and simplicity and freedom that were ours in Eden. We have botched the whole business. We snatched at an illusion, thinking to trade off our innocence for a knowledge only the gods can handle, and it all went to smash in our hands. We would have perished forthwith unless Mercy had clothed us and exiled us from the stark splendor of this godlike knowledge. But we found it was not just a matter of returning to where we had been before our attempted bargain: not only did we lose the bargain itself, but we lost what we had brought with us *to* that bargain; namely, our innocence (and with it the possibility of naturalness, simplicity, and freedom)—so that we were completely pauperized. It wasn't just a matter of going home having been outbidded: we were ruined. The fiend took everything and left us with unnaturalness, complexity, and bondage.

We lost with all of this our lovely nakedness. Suddenly we wanted aprons. Not hats, it might be observed, or gloves: odd business that, right there at the beginning, long before any institutions or traditions or conventions had had time to load us down with guilt-feelings; it almost looks as though the guilt were there before the traditions, which is the opposite of what we hear nowadays. We lost our nakedness—that is, our ability to present ourselves entirely openly to all other selves or to bear their opening of themselves to us. Something had gone wrong. The state of affairs where there was no shame had been mangled, and now privacy was somehow necessary. Shame, like our aprons and our exile, was a shield against our being scorched by unveiled, stark reality. For the nakedness of the other person is the unveiled, stark reality of that person. In Eden it is possible to gaze on this freely.

If this is true, then down with all nude sculpture, all nude swimming, all locker rooms, and so forth. Right?

Wrong. The point is not that we can never

tolerate any nakedness except our own. Rather, it is that we mortals ordinarily find that we need protection in the form of clothes, or doors, or polite conventions for our frailty. As Adam, surely the most splendid man ever, felt he needed cover, and as all men everywhere feel they want to slink away from the group to answer the "call of nature," so we need covering for our nakedness in the general run of daily business.

Our shame over the nakedness of our bodies, then, is itself only a sign of our awareness that we cannot, in this post-Eden realm, sustain total openness with each other. We have lost that lovely freedom and must win our way back to it slowly and painstakingly, a step at a time as it were. We can only begin revealing ourselves in limited situations, both psychologically and physically: psychologically with friends, confessors, or spouses; physically in the nursery where our nakedness is clothed in innocence, then in gyms and camps with others of our own sex where nothing is at stake, then with our spouse, where the great experiment towards freedom really begins in earnest, sheltered with the palisades of fidelity and trust.

The modern experiment in public nudity, it might be observed here, is an effort towards asserting this trust on a wide scale, the idea being, "We'll all affirm this mutual confidence. I have nothing to hide from you, and I will accept the same openness from you. What freedom! How exhilarating!" And it is exhilarating. The hilarious liberty of a summer's day at a woodland pool, with everyone frolicking in his Edenic glory, cannot be gainsaid. The difficulty is that this ordering of things has never furnished a stable pattern for a *society*. It spills relentlessly over into the Dionysian every time, and on the far side of the Dionysian stands surfeit and ennui: there are no surprises left, no discoveries, nothing new and exciting and fresh. The quiver and tingle that naivete alone experiences has long since been drowned in this surfeit. We can't *handle* it. That is the point.

This loss of freedom is behind our closing the bathroom door. For there we are engaged in tasks that reveal our total vulnerability and mortality, and these are things we cannot, in the ordinary run of things, share with everybody. We are precisely too vulnerable. Hearty experiments in communal living, with everything wide open, come back around sooner or later to accepting the notion of some privacy. It is too taxing to be totally open, all the time, with everybody. Dear God—I need to get *alone!*

And our lament is a faithful barometer here: our feelings know when the weather is too sultry or tempestuous. The plain need to close the door is the whole story in capsule: Paradise Lost in one little act.

Most men, though, have spent time in the military or at some sort of camp. None of this punctilious privacy is observed in those places, and nobody seems to be the worse for it. Doesn't this contradict all this about our frailty? We *can*, obviously, be totally open. There aren't even any partitions in most barracks and camp latrines.

But a moment's thought will put this in perspective. We need only ask what happens when a man begins to attain some seniority. What is the first token of that seniority? Privilege. What privilege? Privacy. A room of your own. A latrine with stalls, shared by a few other senior men. Then, when you are the colonel, or the camp director—ah! Your *own* bathroom! For the masses—the recruits and campers—it is a matter of learning to make do in a situation designed for maximum efficiency. This is the same necessity that makes "chow" or "mess" out of food, namely efficiency, not humanness. It is nobody's ideal. You have to put up with it, and if you rise in the ranks you will get the reward: the NCO's quarters; the counsellors' table; the staff latrine.

We close the bathroom door, then; and in so doing, we declare our membership in the exiled race of Adam. But is the closed door the only thing to be observed about the bathroom? Suppose we grant the collective wisdom of the race in having privacy here. We haven't said much about the rite itself that needs to be thus hidden.

And here we may well say, Oh dear. We have managed so far to get through the discussion without being too clinical. Must we now peer at the details? Oh dear.

What makes us anxious here is that in this particular discussion we are trying to grasp the significance of ordinary things, and we hesitate over what it might all mean. We are reluctant to let our *imaginations* play over the data. Doctors and psychologists and researchers may suspend their imaginations, as it were, when they talk about the big things—sex and death and pathology, for example. They can shift into a strictly clinical frame of mind so that they can get on with their job and not be harried by lust or terror or nausea, which are the ordinary responses of our imaginations to sex and death and pathology. Lithe bodies, or dead bodies, or diseased bodies are not neutral data to our imaginations: people who handle them have to set their imaginations in neutral while they work.

But in this discussion we are speaking precisely to our imaginations, since it is by means of imagination that we grasp the kind of significance we are pursuing. Straight science, for example, can speak in a monotone about death, but when we try to come at the *significance* of death and call up our imaginations for the task, we end up with elegies and requiems instead of the clinical monotone. Or again, engineering can tell us how to build walls and hold up a roof, but when we try to respond adequately to what the builder had in mind in erecting Tintern Abbey or Chartres or the Parthenon, we call on our imaginations and end up with poetry.

Not that we are about to have a sonnet on tubs and toilets here. But, short of poetry or prophecy, what ought we to say about the rite that occurs inside the closed door of the bathroom, this rite that we feel should not be public?

Does it not all have to do with *cleansing*? Skin, teeth, digestive system, hair—what else goes on in there? The three porcelain fixtures are, really, *lavers*, designed to make the removal of impurity as convenient as possible for us. There is always something collecting on us or in us that should not stay there, and the task of removing it is a perpetual task. As the priests had to be forever washing and purifying both themselves and everything else, so we find that we have to be at it morning and night and innumerable times in between. If we stop for very long, something gets matted or grimy or clogged. It is a fight, and it goes on to the bitter end.

It is as though we are forced to tend the body in sorrow, as Adam had to till the soil. Uncleanness and decay, mortality and chaos are there, tirelessly assailing the garden (the body as a walled garden is an old idea), reminding us of our frailty and vulnerability and shame. For it is to our shame that we amass impurity and decay: it is an acute reminder of our guilt. Just as the greatest saints have to return daily to their spiritual ablutions, so even the healthiest among us have to be daily at our physical ablutions. Ablution needs to be taken care of in private, as it were, since our sins and our impurities unfit us to hold concourse with others. We have to wash and purge ourselves and *then* go forth to greet our brothers and sisters and fathers and mothers, the idea being that human intercourse is such a high and holy thing that we must be as pure as we can for it. It won't do, for example, to be breathing the miasma from teeth full of rotted food into the face of our friend: it is a stench and must be purged with the strongest dentifrice. By the same token, it won't do to be radiating wrath or lust or envy in company: it is a stench and must be purged by the strongest acts of penitence. We must at least *try* to be arrayed in purity when we approach other selves made in the awe-full image of God. They are most holy creatures. We are most holy creatures. Our intercourse is holy. Dirt and dandruff and sweat and sin mar that intercourse.

It was surely an ancient and gracious wisdom that set the lavers out of sight.

9

The bedroom is the room of beginnings and endings. Here we are conceived, here we are born, here we sleep, and here we die. (That hospitals have now taken birth and death from the household is, like packaged food and air conditioning, convenient but also, somehow, alarming. There lurks in our imagination the hunch that this is not how it should be. The bedroom seems to be the place where these beginnings and endings should occur.)

Conception first. A beginning; but also an end, a consummation. The beginning of life, and the consummation of love. "In my end is my beginning," said Mary, Queen of Scots, and we can see this paradox of beginnings and endings almost anywhere we look. The corn dying so that the ear may be born; the student at his graduation simultaneously finishing and starting; the baby's birth being at once the end of the only world he has ever known and the beginning of a new one; or a Christian's baptism into Christ's death signalling also the beginning of life. All of these are simultaneous beginnings and endings.

The event (conception) which generates our life in the bedroom is such a beginning, for it is at the same time the end (consummation) of love. Here this man and this woman seal the bond towards which they have been moving ever since they first fell in love. Their smiles, their laughter, their small acts of generosity towards each other, their whispers and pledges and plans, their embracing and joy in each other—these have all heralded the consummation towards which they have moved; namely, union. The day when their flesh would become one flesh.

For in this end, this consummation, there is born a new being, made of the flesh of this man and this woman. And the whole point of this new being, this "one flesh" that Scripture talks about is that it will manifest to us all, in visible, daily terms, what Charity looks like. The coming together of these two individuals, and their submission to each other—their "death," in a word, to their right to be independent, private, and autonomous creatures—has brought forth this new being in whose glorious and holy flesh we may see the mysteries of Charity at work—the absurdities that we have already seen at work in all the other rooms of the house: self-giving as the way towards self-discovery, and obedience as mastery, and life springing up from life laid down. My Life For Yours.

And in the rite of conception, we can see, as we have seen in a dozen other exchanges and acts around the house, the whole story in one little act. Here life is "laid down" quite dramatically, in order that the life of love may be born anew, and that literal new life may come into being. The exactness of the picture is astonishing, not to say amusing: both bodies laid down, like the corn of wheat; both laid open, like the corn of wheat. Vulnerability, defenselessness, giving and receiving—nay, giving and receiving wholly indistinguishable from each other, for who will keep tally in these blissful exchanges to make sure the score is even? My life laid down for you; our two lives laid down, becoming one life, and in this laying down and union, lo, the springing forth of new life. My service to you turning out to be joy. Your life laid down for me turning out to be joy. Your acceptance of me being itself your gift to me.

And so on, around and around. The phrases fall over one another and double back on themselves, for what can words do to catch and set forth the mystery of joy from mutually laid-down life, seen so vividly in the rite of conception? Just as the words of the psalmist ("O that men would praise the Lord . . .") or the apostle ("O the depths . . .") or the Church itself ("Sing my tongue the mystery telling . . .") fail when they set about the task of uttering the divine mysteries, so here they stagger under their task. How can we show how this most common of all human commonplaces is also the rarest of treasures? How can we tell of the high mysteries of exchanged life that it dramatizes every time?

But of course second thoughts come hurrying along in the train of a paean like this. What about rape and fornication and adultery and all that? Or what about the plain breakdown in good marriages, where trouble, frustration, and anguish mark the attempt at this rite we are singing so loftily about? What about that? That, surely, is no picture of blissful mysteries.

And would we not have to say here, as we do over every breakdown and trouble in all our mortal experience, that we never do get things quite right, and that we will always find breakdown and trouble attending the good? The ideal eludes us.

For example, Jews and Christians believe that we are made in the image of God; but nearly all of us experience in our own bodies some spoliation of that image: migraines, poor teeth, paralysis, pain, fat, or wrinkles. Even athletes or ballet dancers, whose bodies are as Apollonian as any we men can hope to see, have warts or scars somewhere. What is the matter here? Is the doctrine (that we are made in the image of God) false? No, we say: we *are* made in the image of God, but that ideal is marred and smudged here. Or again, Christians believe that the Church is the Bride of Christ, but as often as not she looks more like the Whore of Babylon. What shall we say? Do we not have to bow our heads sorrowfully and confess, Yes, she has committed whoredoms, but nonetheless that Bride will be presented to her Bridegroom one day without spot or wrinkle.

And so forth. Things are botched and muddled here, one way or another. And this lovely sexual picture of what real Charity is all about—it too is subject to this same botching and muddling. We mishandle sex, for example, as we mishandled things in Eden when we snatched them for our own uses, and that mishandling is called desecration: the holy has been profaned and sorrow is the result. In the sexual realm, this desecration is called rape, fornication, or adultery. The good thing torn out of the holy place and sold in the market. The fruit gobbled in disobedience. Of course it tastes good (God made it, after all); of course the serpent is telling the truth when he says it is good to eat.

The difficulty is that he has left out one crucial part of the story—that you can't ignore the rules in the holy place.

But is it not here as it is all through our experience, that weakness and limitation and sickness and trouble *do* mar the picture, and that we *do* live with headaches and withered limbs and sterility? "Man is born to trouble," said Job's friend Eliphaz, and we try to patch it up with aspirin and crutches and drugs and counselling, and get on with things as well as we can.

The taboos that surround this sexual rite in every tribe and civilization are there because we men know there is more at stake in this little exchange than just the whim of the moment, and that therefore we can't just fiddle or traffic with it. Pagans, Moslems, Hindus, Jews, and Christians, and everyone else, know that something is going on that reaches further than the mere contact of skin on skin. However other cults and religions may have hedged it all with taboo, Judaism and Christianity have set it about with exceedingly high hedges, believing as they do that sexuality is rooted in the design of Creation, and that it speaks to us of the highest mysteries.

One of the taboos, for example, has been that complete sexual union does not rightly occur outside the bonds of fidelity. "Forsaking all other," says the Christian marriage rite. The idea has been that the man and the woman keep themselves exclusively for each other, at least on this level of things. Why? Is their union some privileged society that discriminates against all the rest of us?

Well, yes, in a word. It is privileged and it does discriminate. The only one who has the privilege of entering into that particular shrine (the body of the other) is the priest who has pledged his faithfulness to that shrine alone. But again, why? Why can't we all share the privileges?

Is it not at least partly because the thing which is going on there is, as it were, the most advanced lesson in Charity, and as such must be entered upon by two who will entrust themselves wholly to each other, since Charity asks, eventually, the total giving of ourselves to the other—and we can't do this piecemeal? That is, if I am farming myself out here and there and the other place, then it is obviously not my total self I am giving. The case of the person who "gives himself" wholly to an aged parent, say, or to the poor in a ghetto, or to his students is different, of course: he is giving himself in service for the sake of these others, but not in the special form that is asked of him in the sexual rite. That particular form of giving asks that he open himself up to the other (his spouse) in a unique way. It is to be on all levels—emotional, psychological, spiritual, physical—and that is a demand that must be unique since he cannot bear this kind of vulnerability except with one other who is bound to him with the same kind of trust as he has placed in her.

The obvious question here would be, But we don't see why you are raising the *physical* union to such high stakes. Surely I don't have to pretend to give myself wholly to somebody else just to enjoy one night of pleasure, say. Why can't we both agree to give just thus much of ourselves for just these hours?

And the only answer to this most plausible of questions is, Because the imagery matters. The what? The imagery—that is, the relationship between the external, physical act and the significance of that act. We can't fiddle with things that have implications like this. And we come back around to the beginning; namely, the awareness of all men that the physical, most especially the sexual, *is* in fact the vehicle of significances vastly beyond the momentary act. The people who have denied this (the citizens of Babylon and Sodom, and the editors of *Playboy* and *Playgirl*) have not proved their point.

So the rite is a privileged one, reserved exclusively for the one priest who has pledged himself to faithful attendance on this shrine. And it thus discriminates against all the rest of us who *aren't* pledged to this shrine in this special way. But like all the discriminating that surrounds the holy things, it is paradoxically almost the opposite from the kind of discriminating we get in politics which usually implies oppression or injustice. Here in these mysteries, we see rather the idea of something being "set apart" (the Tabernacle; the sacrifices; the household) for a special work of ministry. As the fenced Tabernacle, and the purged sacrifices, and the walled household are all "for the sake of" something, so this set-apart union of the man and the woman has as its purpose the springing forth of a new being in Love, the "one flesh" spoken of in Eden.

Furthermore, the Jewish and Christian idea in this exclusive union has been, generally, that it will be lifelong. Where that "lifelong" breaks down in divorce, say, we have just that: a "breakdown"; the breakdown was not the idea in the original union, any more than it is in a piece of machinery or in the human body. If it happens, something has gone *wrong*, and we have to salvage what we can. For Christians, the reason why it is ordinarily assumed that a marriage will go on "till death do us part" has been that this advanced lesson in Charity which marriage opens onto is a long, a difficult one, and the life span that my spouse and I are allowed will certainly not be nearly long enough to finish the lesson. It is the same as the reason for the exclusiveness, or monogamy, that we were just talking about; I will have as much as I can do to learn this advanced lesson well with *one* other person; a harem will only confuse my efforts.

Again, Jewish and Christian tradition has accepted taboos that seem to pen marriage in to one *kind* of sexual union; namely, union with another human being (as opposed to an animal, say), and further, with a human being who embodies the *other* aspect of the image of God (i.e., a man marries a woman, not another man, etc.). Why is this?

The idea would doubtless go something like this: when God created humanity in his own image, he made that image appear under a dual mode, man and woman. It seems to have been his idea (at least on the biblical accounting, which is what Jews and Christians hark back to) that we would see that image made whole somehow in the coming together of those two modes. We can see this same kind of thing, of course, anywhere we look. It is not something peculiar to human sexuality. You need stamen and pistil, for example, not two stamens, to keep flowers going. You need night and day to make one whole twenty-four hour unit, not two nights. You need ball and socket, or piston and cylinder, or mortise and tenon, and so forth: everywhere we look we see this functioning together in one harmony of two things that meet the *other* in order for the work to go on. You get a crash or a struggle or at best a mere juxtaposition when you try to get a union out of two things that are identical. Jews and Christians (and, it seems, the rest of humanity as well) would see this same obvious thing at work in the human scene: you need the one (the woman) and the other (the man) to get a true union, and that is what marriage has been understood to be.

Hence, the departures from this theme have been taboo for Jews and Christians. Two men or two women, for example: sexual activity is possible in these situations, but the ancient view would not see it to be quite a successful image of the thing that marriage is supposed to exhibit to us; namely, the one whole flesh—the image of God, really—of which man and woman are the two modes. It would only be the juxtaposition of two mirror images of each other. Or again, a man and a beast: sexual activity is possible here too, but in this case the otherness is too drastic. No real union at all is possible, any more than you can have a union between an oak and a sea serpent, or an aardvark and a hummingbird. The difference is too great. The two do not participate closely enough in any one whole which can be gained by their coming together sexually, and hence it is confusion. You get only monsters. Or again, a man and himself: sexual activity is possible here, but it is only a solitude and hence not really a successful image of *union*. And yet again, a man and his sister or his mother, say: here the two would be too close together to begin with for this necessary otherness to come into play. They already participate in the "one flesh."

And so on with the other variations on the theme. They have been excluded by taboos whose job is, presumably, to help crowd us along towards the Real Thing that the sexual picture is all about; namely, Charity. Self-giving. My Life For Yours. All of it carried on in obedience to the design for the picture, which is that the two aspects of the divine image, the man and the woman, will be united in one whole.

For this act is an important picture of the mystery of divine love. In that love, self-giving turns out to be the way towards joy and freedom, and we have a vivid picture of this in the sexual act. Here the whole thing is a jumble of giving and receiving, all of it transformed into ecstasy; and the ultimate point of self-giving, we might say, is the ultimate point of ecstasy. It is a picture so hilariously vivid that we must either laugh aloud with delight at this divine comedy, or turn away in sheer incredulity— or embarrassment, perhaps, that the high mysteries should be thus served up to us.

Again, this act in which we are conceived in the bedroom has from ancient times been understood to be a form of *knowledge*. "Adam knew his wife," and so forth. This is a piquant irony: here we are, with all of our high notions of ourselves as intellec-

115

tual and spiritual beings, and the most profound form of knowledge for us is a plain business of skin on skin. It is humiliating. When two members of this godlike, cerebral species approach the heights of communion between themselves, what do they do? Think? Speculate? Meditate? No, they take off their clothes. Do they want to get their *brains* together? No. It is the most appalling of ironies: their search for union takes them quite literally in a direction away from where their brains are.

It is too, too ignominious. It is, really, intolerable—*unless* that idea of ourselves as being primarily cerebral or "spiritual" is not quite correct. And no Jew or Christian supposes that it is, since he agrees with God that the Creation was good. For it was earth and water and rocks and wood and flesh and blood, as well as spirit, that sprang forth at the Creation. This, to use a current idiom, was where it was at.

And Christians carry the idea further, believing as they do that God was incarnate in our flesh, thus raising that flesh to the heights of glory. And, more than that, they look for the resurrection of the dead, which seems to imply that the whole story will not be finished until our *flesh* is somehow rescued from the refuse heap of death and restored to its proper place in the harmony of things.

Hence it makes sense that creatures of this sort will, in the furthest reaches of their communion with each other, find it still very much a matter of flesh. The high mysteries seem to be awkwardly attached to plain, visible, touchable things. (A Christian need only remember the two sacraments commanded by the Lord: baptism and the Lord's Supper. They open out onto the most immense vistas in the Divine Drama, and they both are unabashedly physical.)

So sexual union is a form of knowledge. A vivid picture, having something to do, we suppose, with the fact that the true knowledge of the other is much more than an amassing of data about that person. It must be increasingly synonymous with Love, that is, with self-giving, mutuality, and union, as we press further and further in towards the center. (Indeed, if we wish to see the human body as any sort of map of reality, it *is* the center that we press towards in this act!)

But conceiving people is not the only thing that goes on in bedrooms. People are born there too. This is a big enough mystery itself, without anyone's raising the sort of question we have been considering here. Nobody—atheists, sibyls, priests, biochemists, sages, whoever—has the slightest idea how to account for this oddity, really. We can all make an attempt at describing the business, of course: it is the gateway of the soul from the everywhere into the here; it is a routine chemical commonplace of no particular interest; it is a normal function of human anatomy; it is God's gift of a daughter or son to the parents; and so forth. Some at least of these are no doubt true enough. But none of them gets beyond the outer threshold. How we are to connect this business of pregnancy and contractions and placenta with whatever it is about human beings that poets and prophets have tried to get at? It is as daunting a task as trying to say something helpful about death.

For birth, like death, is bang on the frontier between what we can see and what we can't. Science and imagination grope a few inches across that frontier; but even Scripture is oddly silent about the particulars.

What shall we do, then, with this mystery in our bedrooms? Perhaps we ought to drape the room heavily with holy cloths and set censers to smoking and priests to murmuring, if the mystery is really this impenetrable. But no: that is not the way the mysteries come at us in households. In religious sanctuaries, yes; but here they come at us, not in veils and smoke and incantations, but rather in light-of-day, meat-and-potatoes ordinariness. In our routine of common duties, and in our playing and eating and drinking, and in our coupling and giving birth and dying: this is how the mysteries come at us in our households.

So the obvious thing to do is to get on with it. We are doing what we are supposed to be doing with the mysteries when we beget children and bring them forth. The routine goes on and like all the other routines, it is worth doing just for itself.

But it is interesting, if we care to press the inquiry at all, to note that we are brought to the brink when someone arrives in the light of day in our bedroom. They can no more tell us where they came from than a dead person can tell us where he has gone. And we have no time in any case to hear their tales. All is a hurry of sheets, hot water, cloths, blood, and struggle. Nobody has any leisure to ponder the immensities, what with this tot gasping and protesting, and the mother needing to be smoothed out, and the bed cleaned up. If someone were to paw our arm in the middle of all this, trying to get us to ponder the significance of it all, we would have to snap at him, "Let the significance take care of itself." We have to do our reflecting later. We can even read a book about how the mysteries are at work in household routines if we want. But right now we must do our job.

And of course the poor infant has been dragooned willy-nilly into this rite without so much as a by-your-leave from anyone. Here he is, asked to sustain the wreck of the only world he knows, bundled out into daylight and cold air, obliged to start breathing and sucking, and, soon enough, to start working and thinking and suffering. And here are all these people, too, breaking up his lovely solitude. It is a bad business.

But it is what he is made for. Left inside there, he would die. This daylight is for his eyes to open and see. This air is for his lungs to fill themselves with. This earth is for his feet to walk on, and these thoughts are for his brain to go to work on, and these words are for his tongue to start uttering. And these people who have broken into his solitude—they are here to love him and to teach him to love.

For he needs all the help he can get from us. He needs hands to receive him and caress him, and breasts to give him milk, and arms to cradle him, and voices to lull him. Or, let us change the pronouns: *I* need all the help I can get. *I* need to be received and nourished and cradled and lulled. For that infant is I, and you, and Mrs. Smith, and the Emperor of All the Russias. Here we come, out of solitude and dependence, into company and dependence. We didn't know about dependence back in there, but now we begin our lesson.

The lessons begin easily enough, since all I have to do in the early stages is to experience the benefits of others laying down their lives for me. I am asked only to learn the receiving part of the giving/receiving rhythm in this order of exchanged life. Indeed, I can hardly be said to be *learning* it at all, since it never occurs to me in my first year or so that there is any other way possible, much less that there is a part for me to bear waiting for me. If someone told me this, I would fly into a rage and demand my rights. Mutual dependence, as far as I am concerned, is a simple matter of your getting milk and blankets and clean diapers to me pronto. I have to be helped gently towards lessons two, three, and four, where this principle of exchanged life comes gradually into focus as, literally, an *exchange*, so that it means not only Your Life For Mine but also My Life For Yours.

Perhaps one of the earliest lessons in which it begins to come into focus for me is my learning that this nice order of things, with you rushing up at my beck with milk, blankets, and diapers, is, precisely, dependence. That is, I had supposed that this was all automatic—that there was no conceivable alternative, and that it all just *happened*. A few things come slowly into focus: first, that somebody is doing this for me; and next, that I am therefore dependent on them; and next, that it may be costing them something; and next, that this dependence of mine may be acknowledged by uttering the formula "thank you"; and next, by my doing them a good turn.

It doesn't all get phrased in this tidy way, of course. It just comes along in the first two or three years, mostly in a jumble. But this must be more or less the sequence in which the order of exchanged life comes at me. When I am screaming for my milk, it would be hard indeed to get through to me with the advanced lessons in the school—such things as *my* carrying somebody's burden, say, or my interceding in prayer for somebody, or my bearing a cross for somebody. That's nonsense, I scream. And yet these are nothing more than this same scheme of things I am so blithely (or petulantly perhaps) demanding, brought into absolutely clear focus. That is, here is my mother coming to my crib with breasts full of warm milk for me. I think it is automatic and my due. It's all just a comfortable blur so far. What I do not know is that this happy scheme *costs* her something, and that all up and down the line, *everybody's* life depends on exactly this scheme; and that further up the line I may find out that I owe my life to some granny's having prayed for me, or perhaps that I am called upon to pray for someone; and that in the highest reaches of all, the scheme has been dramatized at a place called Golgotha, where One who certainly did not have to do any such thing paid a staggering price for my life simply because he loved me. I don't know yet that I owe my happiness, my comfort, my nourishment, and my life to this woman here at my crib, much less that I, and she, and everyone else owes our eternal life to that Man on that Cross. That's all nonsense—bring me my *milk!*

And the souls in hell are still saying that. We shall have our rights, and we shall have them on our own terms, at our own beck. They are the ones who have refused the lessons, and they indeed have their rights: wrath, boredom, solitude, vanity, and futility.

Whereas the saints in heaven are the ones who, having learned these lessons, now dance solemnly and joyously to the measure that they began to learn back there—now you retreat and I advance (that is, you give the milk and I drink it); now I retreat and you advance (that is, I get breakfast while you sleep in an extra half hour); now we bow, now we embrace, now I lead you, now you step out alone; and always we both obey the steps. My life for yours, my life from yours, yours for mine, yours from mine, joy, joy, joy, praise, thanksgiving, gratitude, alleluia, alleluia, hosanna in *altissimus*, *benedicite omnia opera domini, laudate et superexaltate eum in saeculo,* amen and amen and amen.

Heavens! All this at the childbed? Yes, all this at the childbed. Heaven and hell both coming to the birth with their invitations. And the infant ushered, amongst blood and pain and confusion, into the drama he knows so little of.

But more goes on in bedrooms than conceiving and bringing forth children. We sleep here. Nightly we return here to sink down, supine, as we will one day sink down in our graves. The day has been too much for us. We can't go on without this rest. Just let me lie here, quietly, peacefully. And dear Lord, please don't let the phone ring.

Once more, this rhythm that seems to move in all our experience. Work and play, mountains and valleys, hot and cold, black and white, giving and receiving, activity and rest, sun and shade, man and woman, day and night—all calling back and forth in the lovely antiphons of creation. And this one: after our work, sleep. We are frail, we are mortal, we need to lie down and be renewed. The mightiest heroes and the ruggedest muleteers, despite their strength, have had nightly to lie down because they could not go on unless they did.

Where are we when we are asleep? Poets have tried to get at it, and research teams in universities get huge grants of money to help them find out, and soothsayers have raked through the dreams of kings for auguries, and Sigmund Freud mapped out vast, frightening regions through which we seem to wander when we are lying there. Where are we? Nowhere? Back in infancy? In the womb? Further back in some far, protomythic chasm full of hags, monsters, and scrambled situations? Are there angels standing by? Who knows?

Whatever else we may say about sleep, we know one thing: we are not in control of ourselves when it is upon us. Ghengis Khan himself is as helpless as an infant when he is in his bed, at the mercy of nightmares, thieves, and assassins. Where is the glory of the king when he is in his nightshirt? Where the augustness of the judge in his cap? Where the grace of the noble lady with her hair all tangled like a medusa? There we lie, all of us, serfs, dukes, short order cooks, murderers, and nuns, limp and stupefied. Our regalia is laid aside, our strutting has ceased, our masks are gone. Naked. Vulnerable. Mortal.

This is an odd part of the rite that goes on in households, but, like all the other parts of the rite, it draws us into something that may remind us of how things are. In this case we are obliged to remember with remorseless regularity our mortality. Not just once a year with ashes on our foreheads, but every single night we must admit it.

But it is not just a bleak business of admitting weakness and defeat. Lo and behold, we find that our strength is renewed in these inglorious hours of repose. It is almost as though we have to become as little children, even infants in the womb, and be born again each morning; or as though we die and are raised again each morning to new life. A small, daily reminder of the two great poles between which the thread of our life is strung; an enactment in our ordinary routines of the plain fact that our strength follows after weakness, our manhood after our infancy, our resurrection after our death.

And finally, we die in this room. We return in the

end, as it were, to the bed which received us when we first arrived. Once more we come to the frontier, this time to step across from here to there. The point of our departure for the region from which we get no news, and from which we shall never, never return, is this bed, this couch of our weakness, set here in this room among the things that have attended most closely on our person—our shirts and dresses and shoes, and our belts and earrings and cufflinks, and our emery boards and shoe brushes and fingernail scissors. There they are, on their hangers, in their drawers, or in the little boxes on the bureau where we put them on Thursday evening when we lay down. And now they will sit there on Monday and Tuesday and Wednesday, until someone clears them out, while we—we vanish to where there are no Thursdays or Mondays or any other days. Give us time to collect our wits. Give us a chance to bid proper farewells to these dearest people. Give us time to gird up our loins. Give us time to be shriven . . .

And, like our birth, which would be much more impressive and (we would have thought) appropriate if it had occurred with heralds and processions and great tapestries drawn aside to reveal us there on the balcony, crowned with light, majestic in our innocence—like our birth, which happens instead all in a heap of confusion and rags, so our exit: it ought to be with the high solemnity, dignity, and

126

grace fitting to this august moment when all our accomplishments and our relationships—nay, and our very selves—are caught away altogether and utterly. There ought once more to be trumpeters and pomps. But instead, here we are, rumpled, faded, and gasping; dressed, not in the robes of this high solemnity, but in our pajamas; borne, not in a royal coach, but on this mattress: unable to say a single syllable to these people who so earnestly listen for some sure word of reassurance and farewell from us. We struggle to get in to our life here, and we struggle to get out again. We arrive in a mess and we leave in a mess. Alas, alas, what wretched creatures we are. If this is the way it is, then let us once and for all leave off the silly solemnities with which we deck our lives. We are worms, no more. Our efforts to dignify ourselves and our experience are just so much whistling in the dark.

But this will not do. All men everywhere have known that this will not do. We human beings are not quite satisfied, as dogs or aardvarks are, with this helter-skelter way of arriving and departing. After the flurry we feel we must *do* something. Have a christening. Have a funeral. Something big has happened, and we didn't quite have the leisure to grasp it, and mark it, and come to terms with it in all that huddle of activity. Here—let us solemnize the mystery thus, with white lace and a font and a

127

cake; or with black crepe, a pall and a dirge. One way or another, we must deck the event with tokens that answer somehow to how we feel about it.

And of course for Christians, this exit is much more than just a vanishing into the abyss. We go to God, says the ancient faith. The mightiest mysteries in the whole Drama converge here: death is swallowed up in victory; death has been defeated in the flesh of the Incarnate Word; life now stands beyond the borders of the dark kingdom; instead of dissolution, oblivion, and annihilation, there is resurrection, triumph, and eternal life. The divine immensities with a vengeance.

But here in the bedroom, as in the other rooms in the house, the mystery comes at us piecemeal, hurried along in the plain garb of ordinariness. Anyone who has ever attended on a death knows that when the final hours come, we are down to trivial, trivial items: the window open another inch or two here, a pillow under his shoulder there, or a hanky to wipe his face with. But these, like the saucepans in the kitchen or the drain in the tub or the cushions on the sofa, are vessels in the service of the rite that is celebrated in the house. The great eucharistic mysteries of Charity are all there— obedience and freedom; rules and liberty; self-giving and fulfillment; life from death; sacrifice and oblation; My Life For Yours—observed and enacted in the common routines of this house.